Letting Go & Letting God

21 Centuries of Faith

Kathleen Atkinson, OSB

Liguori
LIGUORI, MISSOURI

Imprimi Potest:
Harry Grile, CSsR, Provincial
Denver Province, The Redemptorists

Published by Liguori Publications
Liguori, Missouri 63057

To order, call 800-325-9521
www.liguori.org

Library of Congress Cataloging-in-Publication Data

Atkinson, Kathleen.
  Letting go and letting God : 21 centuries of faith / Kathleen Atkinson, OSB. -- First Edition.
    pages cm
  1. Catholics--Biography. 2. Christian biography. 3. Catholic Church--History. 4. Church history. I. Title.
  BX4651.3.A85 2013
  282.092'2--dc23
  [B]
                                          2013002319

pISBN: 978-0-7648-2197-4
eISBN: 978-0-7648-2309-1

Liguori Publications, a nonprofit corporation, is an apostolate of The Redemptorists. To learn more about The Redemptorists, visit Redemptorists.com.

Printed in the United States of America
17 16 15 14 13 / 5 4 3 2 1
First Edition

Table of Contents

With gratitude

To Marjory and Myron Atkinson,
my parents, who have inspired me with their faithfulness
and taught me to live passionately and generously.

To the men and women
throughout the centuries who have stepped out in faith,
been unafraid to live on the margins, and remind us
not to compromise this one brief life we have been given.

Foreword

One of my favorite passages in Scripture is the story of Moses and the burning bush. The story tells us that Moses was in awe of the amazing sight before him—a bush on fire but not consumed by the flames. Moses had never seen anything like that. God certainly got his attention, but God wanted more from him. God wanted Moses to remove his shoes and to realize that the very place where he was standing was holy ground. The ground was holy because God was alive within Moses, not just in the burning bush. It was important for Moses to realize God's presence within him before God invited him to lead the Israelites out of slavery and into freedom. God was setting a huge challenge before Moses, and Moses was understandably not very enthusiastic about approaching Pharaoh and demanding he set his slaves free. God, however, patiently responded to all of Moses' fears, assuring him that he would be guided, protected, and directed by God's love and support. God promised to be with him and within him, just as God was within the burning bush.

When I finished reading this amazing book by Sister Kathleen Atkinson, I realized that she is serving just as God did with Moses and the burning bush. By introducing the reader to twenty spiritual giants who were remarkable in their courage, faithful in their service, and passionate in their love for God, Kathleen also introduces us to the compassion, justice, and integrity that are possible in our own time. By choosing one person from each of the past twenty centuries to inspire us and fill us with awe at their faithfulness to God's call, she then challenges us to be spiritual leaders for the twenty-first century. Kathleen invites us to believe that the same God who worked wonders in the lives of the great saints from the past is now living inside us and is ready, willing, and able to empower us to be servant leaders of the present. Perhaps our initial response will be similar to that of

Moses. Like him, we could be filled with fear and resistance. May we, like Moses, come to discover that God is burning within us and that "with God, all things are possible."

Kathleen Atkinson has a gift of communicating God's love in a clear, creative, and compelling way. She is deeply aware that life is not always easy and can be filled with personal, relational, and global pain. She is also deeply aware that "God is always there" (the title of her first book) and knows intimately that God's presence will never burn out.

This book can be a valuable resource for personal growth, adult faith-formation programs, religious education for youth, or spiritual retreats. May it serve as a source of inspiration and challenge for you so you can discover *your* place among the communion of saints.

Sister Jean Maher, OSB
Director of McCabe Renewal Center
Duluth, Minnesota

Introduction

I n June 1992, I was teaching vacation Bible school in a small town in North Dakota. Between a small communication discrepancy and my own poor planning, I found myself arriving just three days after I had returned from a month-long mission trip to Guatemala with college students. I was tired!

After teaching that first day, I returned to the home where I was staying and fell sound asleep on the bed. Hearing the door open and the soft giggle of two kindergarten girls, I thought, *I'll keep my eyes closed and they'll leave.* Instead, they came closer and closer, and I realized they were gently strewing lilac petals around and over me as I lay there. They tiptoed and whispered and dropped these fragrant petals as if anointing me in my rest. They didn't expect me to wake up and respond. They didn't explain in words what they were doing, and they didn't wait and watch for my response. They simply tiptoed out and closed the door again. I lay there anointed, gradually awakening to the new reality around me.

This same gradual awakening has brought me to an awareness of our long tradition of men and women who have encouraged people to "wake up" and live their faith boldly. Some of them, like Gregory the Great, lived at crucial times in the history of the Church and the world. Their impact was immediate, and their names well known through the ages. Others, such as Kateri Tekakwitha, lived virtually unremarkable lives, anonymous at the time but still faithfully walking the Christian journey day by day. All of their lives take root in particular cultures and historical contexts, yet each one offers us universal truths.

In this book, I have chosen one person from each century to be featured. A few of their life spans overlap because some periods of history were flourishing times for mystics, missionaries, and saints, while other times were undistinguished. I attempted to balance male and female personalities, various ethnicities and economic backgrounds, people who were actively involved in the world around them and those who were inner travelers from their monastic cell. By writing this book, I was not seeking to write extensive biographies or theological analyses of individuals but, instead, to highlight lives that challenge us today. The prayer and reflection questions in each chapter invite you to connect your own twenty-first–century life with that of another time and place. My hope is that you will gently awaken to a person or persons with whom you feel a kinship and be inspired to live your own life just a little more daringly.

Mary Magdalene
Apostle to the Apostles

Jesus said to her,
  "Do not hold on to me."
I was once certain
  of so many things—

Certain
  of light and dark
  life and death
  filled and empty
  hatred and love.

I was once certain
  of so many things—

  but grief broke me open
  and they tumbled out
  as one jumbled mess.

Certainty
  tumbled out
  among them.

Shutterstock: Mary of Magdala, El Greco

Mary Magdalene, or Mary of Magdala, could almost be called the "saint of uncertainty." Pope Gregory the Great first suggested that she was a prostitute in a homily about Luke's Gospel in 591. For centuries this portrayal was promoted by homilists, writers, and artists. The *Lateran Missal* combined Mary Magdalene with Mary of Bethany; theologians such as Augustine and Thomas Aquinas left the question unresolved; while the Greeks distinguished between the two and established two different feasts.

In 1969, Pope Paul VI separated Luke's sinful woman, Mary of Bethany, from Mary of Magdala in the arrangement of the *Roman Missal*. However, misidentification continues even in contemporary media, such as Andrew Lloyd Webber's *Jesus Christ Superstar* and Mel Gibson's *The Passion of Christ*. It is perpetuated with the designation of Mary Magdalene as the patron of penitent sinners, wayward women, hairdressers, and perfume makers.

Mary Magdalene could also be called the "saint of certainty," the Apostle to the Apostles. The four gospels have little to say about her before the crucifixion other than Luke, who names her as one of the women who traveled with Jesus and who had been healed of evil spirits and infirmities. She came into prominence as a witness to the key events of our Christian faith: Mary Magdalene stands faithful at the crucifixion, is the first to discover the empty tomb, and the first to encounter the risen Christ. Mary Magdalene is the first to announce the good news of Jesus' resurrection to the other disciples and to invite them to come with her to witness this great event. Though others fled, Mary courageously remained, certain that Jesus was the Messiah, certain that he had risen from the dead.

Mary of Magdala's prominence in the gospels and early Church tradition support her role as a recognized disciple and leader within the Christian movement. Two streams of tradition (more uncertainty!) speak of her latter years. One tradition suggests she retired to Ephesus with Mary, the Mother of Jesus, and John, the beloved disciple. The other follows a popular devotion that holds that Mary, her brother Lazarus, and several companions fled the persecutions in the Holy Land in a flimsy boat without mast or rudder. They traveled across the Mediterranean Sea, landing at a place called Saintes-Maries-de-la-Mer near Arles. According to French tradition, Mary Magdalene converted the entire population of Provence and then spent her last days alone in penance and prayer in the wilderness. Her relics are believed to lie in a small crypt in the Basilica of St. Maximin, in Provence. Her date of death is not known, but her feast has been celebrated on July 22 since the tenth century.

Prayer

Jesus,
    I'm afraid of resurrection.
I want life back as I remember it
    in some easier, more certain past.
I'm tempted to keep you as a warm familiar memory,
    yet I hear your command not to cling.
Help me to say YES to life in each moment
    and to you, my risen Lord. Amen.

Connecting With Mary of Magdala

"Do not hold on to me" (John 20:17) says the risen Christ to Mary Magdalene outside the empty tomb. He does not say not to "touch" him, as had been presented in older translations of Scripture, but do not "hold on to" him. Do not cling, clutch, grasp Jesus as he appeared to her at that moment. Resurrection is no time to live in the past. Jesus must ascend to the Father, and Mary must go and tell the others that he is truly risen.

It's easy to imagine the struggle Mary Magdalene must have faced. She had hoped the Jesus she knew was back as she remembered him before he was crucified. Failing that, she was settling for a corpse she could anoint, a grave she could visit, a place where she could weep and grieve and rejoice and heal all that had happened during their time together. This is why Mary Magdalene was at the tomb that morning in the first place; she certainly was not expecting to meet Jesus, of all people!

We struggle in the same way. Jesus is alive and goes ahead of us; we cannot hold him back. We cannot hold him in a tomb of stone nor in certitude of doctrine nor in righteousness of action. We cannot demand that he conform to our ways of thinking; Jesus doesn't even conform to the expectation of staying dead!

As if resurrection was not scandalous enough, Jesus sent a woman to announce the Good News. The apostles were hiding, the officials were engaged in public-relations damage control, and the marginalized were being called by name—"Mary."

We, too, are called by name. We are called to stand faithfully at the foot of the cross and in the midst of the suffering of our world. We are called to go to the places of seeming death and be broken open to receive new life. We are called to proclaim a message to the frightened, the defensive, the pretentious, the marginalized.

We are called. Do not hold back.

Reflect and Pray

✣ When have you experienced the breaking-open grief of Mary at the tomb? Reread the poem at the beginning of this chapter; what invitation from the Lord do you hear through these words?

✣ What does resurrection mean to you at this time of your life?

✣ To whom are you being called to go and tell the Good News? What message are you called to proclaim?

Ignatius of Antioch
50–107 (c)

*I am God's wheat,
and I am to be ground
by the teeth of wild beasts
so that I may become
the pure bread of Christ.*

"I am God's wheat," Ignatius wrote in his Letter to the Romans as he declared his willingness to die for God's sake.

"I am God's wheat…" Ignatius lived as he poured himself out in efforts to inspire hope and courage amidst the terrors of persecution.

"I am God's wheat," Ignatius prayed as he journeyed to Rome, there to become the food of wild beasts and a circus spectacle for the people.

Shutterstock: History of the Church, circa 1880

I gnatius of Antioch was born in Syria around the year 50. Little is known about his early life; what we do know comes primarily from the seven letters he wrote while on his way to Rome to be martyred.

He was among the disciples of John the Evangelist, therefore part of the second generation of Jesus' followers at a time when the Church was rapidly developing. Ignatius was the third bishop of Antioch in Roman Syria, and it is a well-documented belief that Saint Peter himself consecrated Ignatius as the immediate successor of Evodius in this all-important See. It was in Antioch, after all, that the disciples were first named "Christian."

Life was harsh and brutal in mid first-century Rome, and an overwhelming sense of powerlessness led people to look for someone to blame. Nero found his scapegoat in the Christian community of Rome, and Domitian found his in the Christians of Syria. The Emperor Trajan sought to end all the so-called secret societies; his greatest fear was the burgeoning Christian movement with their new and different way of life.

Trajan's method was to decree that all people must join together in the worship of pagan gods; refusing to do so was punishable by death. But Ignatius courageously defied the emperor's edict and encouraged his followers to do likewise. According to the account inscribed at a memorial of his martyrdom, his bearing before Trajan was characterized by inspired eloquence, sublime courage, and even a spirit of exultation. It was during this interview before Trajan that Ignatius first referred to himself as Theophorus, ancient Greek for "God-bearer."

The emperor ordered Ignatius to be put in chains and taken to Rome, where he would be fed to the lions of the circus. Apparently, this was a precautionary step, as it was feared the Christians would revolt if he was martyred in Antioch. The trip passed through Asia Minor and Greece, thus allowing many in the smaller towns and villages at last to see the famous Ignatius. Rather than instill fear of a similar fate, Ignatius's example inspired and encouraged many early Christians.

During the several months' journey, Ignatius wrote letters to the Ephesians, Romans, and other Christian communities. He pleaded with them to remain in harmony with their bishops. Also, he was the first to use the Greek word *katholikos*, meaning "universal," "complete," and "whole" to describe the Church. Calling them "fellow travelers on the road to God," Ignatius reminded these communities that Jesus' Incarnation gave special value to what they did in their everyday lives.

As he neared Rome, the bishop feared there would be a movement among the more influential of his followers to obtain a mitigation of his sentence. Ignatius pleaded with them to do nothing to prevent his winning the crown of martyrdom. As he faced his own death, he was particularly focused on imitating Jesus' own suffering, writing, "If I suffer, I shall be emancipated by Jesus Christ; and united to him, I shall rise in freedom" (Ignatius' Letter to the Romans, 4:3).

According to legend, Ignatius arrived in Rome on December 20, the last day of the public games. Hurried off to the Flavian Amphitheater, Ignatius was released to ferocious lions and immediately devoured, completing his earthly life.

"I am writing to all the Churches and I enjoin all, that I am dying willingly for God's sake, if only you do not do me an untimely kindness. Allow me to be eaten by the beasts, which are my way of reaching to God. I am God's wheat, and I am to be ground by the teeth of wild beasts, so that I may become the pure bread of Christ" (Ignatius' Letter to the Romans, 4:1*).*

Prayer

Teach me, O Lord, what it means to completely surrender.
Lead me where you want me to go
    strip me of all vanity and status
    and let me be broken, shared, and poured out for others.
Lead me beyond my wildest dreams,
    for "I am God's wheat."

Connecting With Ignatius of Antioch

The late great conductor Leonard Bernstein was once asked which instrument in the orchestra was the most difficult to play. The maestro gave an immediate and surprising answer. "Second fiddle," he said. "I can get plenty of first violinists. But to find someone who can play second fiddle with enthusiasm—that's a problem. Yet if there is no one to play second fiddle, there is no harmony."

In an age of self-aggrandizement, popularized by social-media and reality-television shows, the story of Ignatius of Antioch challenges Christians to reflect seriously on their role as followers. This follower of Jesus did not draw attention to his own suffering, to his status as bishop, or to his eloquence of discourse; rather, Ignatius pointed past himself to the love of God.

Ignatius recognized that he was to play second fiddle; he desired to be crushed and lose his individualism to become part of something new and greater.

Seed to wheat.
Wheat to bread.
Bread to nourishment for the world.

Reflect and Pray

♱ Listen to a piece of music and become aware of the harmony. What invitation do you hear in this for your own life?

♱ What are the "wild beasts" that crush your spirit? How can you bring them to Jesus so that new life may come forth?

♱ If you were to write a letter as you approached death, to whom would you want to write? What would you say?

Origen of Alexandria
(185–254)

The physical voice we use in prayer
need not be great nor startling;
even should we not lift up any great cry
or shout, God will yet hear us.

Origen has always been controversial:

His self-mutilation was condemned as an over-zealous misinterpretation of a scriptural text.

He preached without being ordained, and then was ordained in an unauthorized manner.

He was criticized, acclaimed, declared heretical, and named a Father of the Church.

Wikipedia: Illustration from *Les Vrais Pourtraits Et Vies Des Hommes Illustres* by André Thevet

Origen Adamantius ("man of steel") was born near Alexandria in 185, the child prodigy of Leonides. The eldest of seven children in a Christian home, Origen grew up learning the Bible and the importance of virtuous living. When Leonides was thrown into prison during the Severian persecutions of 202–203, Origen sought to join him but was kept from doing so by his mother, who stole his clothing. He wrote an encouraging letter to his father, exhorting him to persevere to martyrdom and promising to care for those left behind. Leonides was beheaded and his wealth confiscated by the government, thus Origen assumed the responsibility of supporting his family. This he did by selling his manuscripts and becoming a teacher at the renowned catechetical school of Alexandria. Saint Jerome wrote that the famous school had been founded by the Apostle Mark. At the time of Origin, it was led by Clement of Alexandria until he was run out of town by followers of Severus.

After Clement had fled, the catechetical school at Alexandria stood empty for a time; Demetrius, Bishop of Alexandria, appointed the eighteen-year-old Origen to reopen the school and assume its leadership. The school taught secular subjects and philosophy in addition to Christian studies and was therefore frequented by pagans as well as Christians. As a result, Origen's school converted many men and women to the Christian faith, producing outstanding catechumens, confessors, and martyrs. The young Origen was known to accompany his students to their martyrdom if that became their destiny, always exhorting them to be courageous as he had his own father.

Origen continued his own studies at the school of the pagan philosopher Ammonius Saccas, conversing with the philosophers to better defend the Christian faith against pagan arguments. He lived an ascetic life, teaching all day and spending most of the night studying the Bible. To avoid scandalizing the pagan Alexandrians by instructing both men and women, he voluntarily had himself castrated, following literally the admonition of Jesus in Matthew 19:12, "For there are eunuchs who have been so from birth, and there are eunuchs who have been made eunuchs by others, and there are eunuchs who have made themselves eunuchs for the sake of the kingdom of heaven. Let anyone accept this who can." In other disciplines of the ascetic life, such as fasting, limited amounts of sleep, and scant possessions, Origen likewise pursued a life of martyrdom that had been denied to him in actual death.

Between 203 and 231, Origen attracted large numbers of students through his manner of living as much as through his teaching. When a wealthy convert supplied Origen with secretaries, he began to write, sometimes dictating to seven different secretaries at the same time. Few authors were as prolific as Origen, as early ecclesiastical writers attributed to him six thousand writings. Later historians placed the number closer to two thousand, which in itself is a vast amount of writing. Titled "the first biblical scholar," his zeal for the study of Scripture drove him to learn Hebrew, study the original texts, and consult Jewish scholars on the Hebrew Testament. Origen analyzed Scripture on three levels: the literal, the moral, and the allegorical. These corresponded to the philosophical dimensions of body, soul, and spirit in ascending order of importance. Furthermore, Origen created a Christian philosophy, synthesizing Greek technique and biblical assumptions.

Like Clement before him, Origen traveled much, both to learn and to teach. His journeys between 213 and 218 included Greece, Palestine, Arabia, Antioch, and Rome. He was asked by Julia Mamaea, the mother of Severus Alexander, to expound Christianity at the Imperial Court. And he became involved in theological disputes throughout the Church, eventually being called upon to adjudicate as a theological expert.

While in Caesarea in 230 he was ordained, which offended his home bishop, Demetrius of Alexandria. Demetrius expelled Origen on the grounds that his ordination defied the authority of the Alexandrian Church and that, as an eunuch, Origen was not allowed to be ordained. Thus Origen remained in Caesarea the rest of his life, vigorously preaching, writing, and living an ascetic life. During the persecutions of Decius (249–251), Origen was imprisoned and tortured, just barely kept alive in the hope that he would renounce his faith. But Decius died first and Origen was set free, though his health was broken; he died in 253, soon after his release from prison.

Three centuries after his death, Origen was declared a heretic at the Council of Constantinople (553). Some contend that Origen was simply attempting to frame the Christian beliefs into the language and context of his day, taking what he had learned from Greek philosophy and integrating it with early Christian teaching, thus building on the foundation created by Clement and under the influence of the Stoics. But with this newly formed basis, he became overconfident and made speculations that were not supported by Scripture. Rather, they overly relied on Plato and other philosophers in the understanding and interpretation of Scripture. Specifically, Origen was condemned for teaching that all spirits were created equal, existed before birth, and then fell from grace. He believed all spirits, even Satan, could be saved and that life is primarily a journey from corruption to the original blessed state. Most notably, Origen was condemned for portraying the Trinity as a hierarchy, not as an equality of Father, Son, and Spirit.

The controversy about Origen continues to this day, nearly nineteen centuries later. Whether a heretic or one of the first great Christian minds, a disobedient fanatic or faithful defender of the Church, Origen was undoubtedly one of the most influential persons of the early Church.

Prayer

Jesus,
   you are the divine Teacher.
Create in me
   the mind to understand your way
   the humility to seek your truth
   the courage to follow your life.
Amen.

Connecting With Origen of Alexandria

Considering our contemporary educational model that stresses accelerated coursework, individual distance learning, and degree attainment as a commodity to benefit one's annual salary, Origen's lifelong pursuit of teaching and learning may seem quite inefficient. His school was grounded in dialogue, reflection, and community. It served as a center for study and peace in a time of persecution and chaos. And its end goal was to open up questions and new avenues of thinking rather than offer clear doctrinal answers. When varying traditions and disciplines of study come together, rather than form specialized conclaves, each person must come with humility and a willingness to be misunderstood. Our fruitful dialogue will bring about shared understanding more than eloquence of speech or exhibition of academic achievement.

We need to learn this approach to reflective dialogue rather than debate today. Origen's community of learners reminds us that this takes time. And his commitment to study reminds us that dialogue is not to be taken lightly. Origen's experience of being criticized, marginalized, erroneous, even tortured, teaches us that to live with passion exacts a cost.

Jesus reminds us that passion also leads to resurrection.

Reflect and Pray

✟ When have you experienced yourself misunderstood or outcast for speaking your understanding of a truth?

✟ Who has been a challenging teacher for you in your faith journey? What did you learn about yourself in the struggle?

✟ What are some challenges in our age of translating the Christian faith to a new generation by words and methods they can understand?

Macrina the Younger
(327–379)

You have released us, O Lord,
from the fear of death.

Living without fear,
even as a woman in the fourth century.
   That was Macrina.

Living without fear,
even when faced with the daunting task
of raising her nine younger siblings.
   That was Macrina.

Living without fear,
even as the abbess of a double monastery.
   That was Macrina.

Living without fear, even the fear of death.
   That was Macrina.

Living without fear
because she lived within Jesus Christ, her Lord.
   That was Macrina.

Wikipedia: Fresco in Saint Sophia Cathedral in Kiev

Macrina the Younger was born in 327, in Caesarea of Cappadocia (now southeastern Turkey). She was the first child of her pious parents, Basil and Emilia. A dream her mother had when she was ready to be delivered inspired her parents to call her Thecla, after Saint Paul's companion, the virgin martyr. However, the rest of the household and her relatives preferred to call her Macrina after her devout grandmother, and that is how she came to be known.

The grandmother, Macrina the Elder, had lived in the days of the Emperor Diocletian, who made a determined effort to destroy the Christian faith. She and her husband fled into hiding and survived into the time of Constantine. Their son, Basil the Elder, and his wife, Emilia, had several distinguished children, most notably Basil the Great, Gregory of Nyssa, Peter of Sebastea, Naucratios, and Dios of Antioch.

Macrina the Younger was the title given to the oldest offspring in this renowned family of Basil and Emilia to distinguish Macrina from her grandmother. Betrothed at the age of twelve, as was the custom of the day, Macrina experienced the death of her fiancé as freedom to pursue her own calling to the spiritual and intellectual life. After the death of her father, Macrina became chiefly responsible for the management of their vast family wealth and the upbringing of her ten younger brothers.

And in all these pursuits, she excelled.

Macrina persuaded her mother to renounce their wealthy lifestyle and help her establish a monastery on their estate. This community of women was renowned for their pious spirituality, artistic talent, scholastic ability, and generosity to the poor. They chose to live simply so as to eliminate the social and economic distinctions that existed between the wealthy patrons and the women they brought into their home for care. They lived under one roof and held everything in common: they ate together, worked together, and prayed together, serving the Lord in oneness of heart and mind.

When Macrina's brothers were tempted to become conceited about their intellectual accomplishments, she deflated them with affectionate but pointed jibes—as only an older sister can. Macrina's example encouraged some of them to found monastic communities for men. For example, Dios founded one of the most celebrated monasteries in Constantinople. And three of them (Basil, Gregory, and Peter) proceeded to become bishops; all of them were leaders for the faith of Nicea against the Arians. Gregory credits Macrina as the spiritual and theological intelligence behind her siblings' notable careers in the Church. He describes her as both beautiful and brilliant, an authoritative spiritual teacher.

Macrina considered no task too demeaning, living and working side by side with the maidservants. Nor did she consider any study or spiritual practice beyond her because of her gender; she was the one who provided the leadership and inspiration for the community of monks organized by Basil. Macrina lived and died as a free woman—free to challenge conventional boundaries; free to lead as a strong woman; free to love without fear, even the fear of death.

Prayer

Jesus, release me from the fear
  that drives me to seek out the approval of others.
Nurture in me the desire to treasure your will above all else.
Guide me to use my talents with a heart that is grateful.
Surround me with holy people who will
  inspire, challenge, and love me.
You have released us, O Lord, from the fear of death.

Connecting With Macrina the Younger

In her life, Macrina was faced with much to fear. She lost her fiancé, which changed the picture of her secure future. She lost her father, which placed her in a position of leadership in a large and wealthy family. Finally, Macrina dared to go against the expected behavior for women of her time to pursue study. She established a monastic community and admonished a bishop (though he was her own brother).

Like Macrina, we all face moments that cause us to feel fear. Often our fears seem perfectly reasonable: "I can't give too much money to the poor; what guarantee do I have that I won't need it in the future?" Sometimes they are tied to our past: "We tried that several years ago, and it didn't work. I'm not trying it again." More often than not, our fears are based on the perceived expectations of other people and the uncertainty of their response to our decision.

We can be certain only of Jesus. His love is unconditional. His desire is for our freedom from all that holds us back from following his will. Though we can choose to cling safely to reason, the past, or the opinion of others, it is essential to understand that today's world needs our gifts and talents.

Macrina teaches us that we are called to release our fears to the Lord and move forward, challenging us from her time and place to be faithful in our own time in the places we find ourselves.

Reflect and Pray

✝ What do you fear? Honestly tell Jesus about it. Listen to what he responds.

✝ Take time for quiet and listen to the deepest desire of your heart. Where do you hear God calling you at this time in your life? What would you do if you were released of all fear?

✝ Macrina was blessed with a family and monastic community that supported her as she sought to follow the Lord's will. List the names of at least three people who are your spiritual support.

Brigid of Kildare
(450–525)

*I would like the angels of heaven
to be among us.
I would like an abundance of peace.
I would like full vessels of charity.
I would like rich treasures of mercy.
I would like cheerfulness to preside over all.
I would like Jesus to be present.*

It takes courage—and an Irishwoman—
   to lay forth her requests in such a way,
   but this was Brigid of Kildare:

Her prayer sings
   and has been memorialized in many a ballad.

Her enthusiasm celebrates
   a playful intimacy with her God.

Her longing exposes
   a heart of compassion for any in need.

Saint Brigid of Kildare, or Brigid of Ireland, was born in Faughart, near Dundalk, County Louth. Several legends are told about her family origins. Some say her father was Dubhthach, an Irish chieftain, and her mother, Brocca, a slave of his court who had been baptized by Saint Patrick. Other sources, however, suggest that Brigid's mother was Portuguese, kidnapped by Irish pirates and brought to Ireland to work as a slave in much the same way as Patrick had been. It's been said that shortly after Brigid's birth, she was sent away to Murroe in East Limerick to be educated within another family until she came of an age to be useful to the household. It has also been suggested that parts of her biography were adapted from the pagan goddess Brigid, the goddess of fire, after whom she was named.

The actual historical details of her life, however, are secondary to the love and veneration held by the Irish people for the woman called "Mary of the Gael." Venerated as a saint in Catholic, Anglican, and Orthodox traditions, Brigid is considered one of Ireland's three patron saints, along with Patrick and Columba. Her feast day, February 1, is the traditional first day of spring in Ireland, thereby perpetually connecting Saint Brigid with the renewal of the earth, the promise of abundance, the hope of new growth, and the eternal cycle of new life.

Inspired by the preaching of Saint Patrick, Brigid consecrated herself to God at an early age. Numerous stories testify to her piety and uninhibited generosity to anyone in need. In fact, many of Brigid's earliest miracles seem to have rescued her from giving something away that belonged to another. Sent with the other young women to collect butter made from the milk of the cows, she gave all of hers to the poor. When restitution was demanded, Brigid was miraculously in possession of the milk she had given away and more. Similarly, as a child she gave a piece of bacon to a dog, only to find it replaced when she was about to be disciplined. She reportedly could never refuse the poor who came to her father's door, dispensing milk, flour, and clothing to all. The saint's unbounded charity angered her father, and when she finally gave away his jewel-encrusted sword to a person with leprosy, Dubhthach realized her disposition was indeed best suited to the life of a nun. Brigid thus finally got her wish and was sent to a convent.

Immediately young women were drawn by Brigid's holiness and joined her. At age fifteen, she and seven others approached Bishop Mel to establish a convent near Croghan Hill. According to legend, when they appeared before him, a fiery flame rose from above Brigid. At Bishop Mel's request, Brigid then founded a convent at Ardagh, the first convent of strict religious observance to be established on Irish soil. She went on to found many more monasteries throughout Ireland. Through them, thousands came to receive instruction in the Christian faith.

Brigid's most famous foundation is at Kildare, the "Church of the Oaks." It was a double monastery, including men and women, with Brigid presiding over both communities. A woman of wisdom and common sense, Brigid's genius for leadership and organization was widely recognized. She established schools, set sisters to work making vestments, and organized the episcopal government of her city. Bishops, priests, chieftains, and kings frequently came to seek her counsel. More than anything else, however, Brigid continued to be renowned for her hospitality, with special regard for the poor and infirm. Kildare became a place of holy pilgrimage for all; from the prominent and powerful to the lowly and forgotten, Abbess Brigid presided, counseled, and served with her very hands-on approach to leadership. Brigid died at the age of seventy-five, but accounts of her miraculous healing and care continue into the present.

Prayer

Jesus, I thank you.
I delight in your abundant gifts of life and love.
Let me not cling to them but overflow to the world.
Let me not be cautious in loving but passionate.
Let me not be guarded in welcome but extravagant.
Let me live and dance and sing with the heart of an Irishwoman
    named Brigid.

Connecting With Brigid of Kildare

The Irish are an oral-based culture filled with great stories, many of which were put to music and sung as ballads. The story of Brigid was transmitted in this way. It is filled with legends that may or may not be accurate in historical detail. It is, however, filled with truth.

Brigid teaches us the truth of God's lavish generosity. Because God has first been so generous, we must do the same. The beauty of nature, in all of its wildness and abundance, serves as a reminder of God's gift. God cannot be tamed or controlled; God will not be bottled up in antiseptic creedal statements nor confined to certain locations deemed sacred. Brigid reminds us that God is Life: creative energy, fiery anointing, wellspring of charity.

Brigid's charity took no stock in prudent financial planning for the future. Revered as the patron saint of Irishwomen and mothers, she embodies the Christian mandate for hospitality. Throughout the centuries, mothers have eaten less so that their children may be fed. They have toiled into the night after the family is asleep and awakened at dawn to prepare for the day. Brigid was an abbess of renowned influence and a distinguished scholar who considered Jesus' command to clothe the naked and feed the hungry to be her greatest calling.

Her story calls us to do the same.

Reflect and Pray

☩ Trusting in God's abundant love and giving, write a litany of desires: "I would like…"

☩ Reflect on the litany you wrote. What are you learning about yourself from it? What do you learn about your priorities and your worldview; your relationship with God?

Gregory the Great
(540–604)

Servant of the Servants of God

A youth of great wealth and power
  yet he considered himself the servant of the servants.

Abbot of the monastery
  yet he considered himself the servant of the servants.

Leader of the Roman Catholic Church
  yet he considered himself the servant of the servants.

Father of the Western Church
  yet he considered himself the servant of the servants.

S. GREGORIVS

Pope Gregory I, popularly known as Gregory the Great, was born in Rome in 540, the son of a Roman senator and administrator of one of the seven regions of Rome. He descended from a long line of Roman nobility with allegiance to the Church: two previous popes were in his family lineage (Felix III and Agapetus I) as well as several nuns.

Gregory served as prefect of the city of Rome from 573–578, responsible for finances, police, and public works. During this time he developed administrative skills that served him well when, upon the death of his father, he distributed his great wealth and turned the family home into a monastery. From this monastery sprang several others, while Gregory committed his energy to the study of Scripture and the rhythm of the monastic life.

His administrative skills did not go unnoticed, however, and in 579, Pelagius II ordained Gregory a deacon and sent him to Constantinople as the Pope's personal emissary. Even as part of the imperial court, Gregory sought to live a monastic life and was elated when he was recalled to Rome in 586 to serve as abbot of the monastery of St. Andrew. In 589 a flood swept through Rome, destroying the grain reserves and instigating a famine. This was followed by a plague that killed many, including Pope Pelagius in 590. Gregory was elected to succeed him, and though reluctant, he went to work with vigor and expertise.

Gregory's first act was to organize penitential processions to the seven churches of Rome to pray for the end of the plague. He then organized systematic relief for the poor refugees who had come to the city. Gregory ordered his clergy to seek out the poor and care for them. He increased production of food on the vast lands that were held by the Church and made distribution to the needy a priority; monks brought food to those who were too ill to collect it themselves. Furthermore, Gregory himself was engaged in the preparation and delivery of food and did not take any for himself until all others were fed.

Gregory then set about reforming the Church itself. He removed Church officials "for pride and misdeed," enforced celibacy, and reorganized the vast wealth of the Church to put it at the disposal of all the baptized rather than the powerful individual clergy. During the thirteen years Gregory served as pope, not only did he reform the Church through his organizational changes, but he was a prolific writer. His *On Pastoral Care*, a handbook for the instruction of bishops, served as a primary manual throughout the Middle Ages. Believing that preaching was one of the clergy's primary duties, Gregory conducted a preaching tour of area churches and published his homilies.

During his papacy Gregory also published his *Dialogues*, a history of the lives of Italian saints. He also made sweeping changes to the Roman liturgy and wrote more than 800 letters to the Eastern churches in an attempt to keep union with Rome. Gregory's appreciation for church music has been recognized by the giving of his name ("Gregorian") to the plainsong chant that he promulgated. In 596 he sent Augustine, along with forty monks, as missionaries to Britain.

Gregory set a high mark for the medieval papacy as a leader of the Church and state. He was the first pope to call himself *Servus Servorum Dei*, "servant of the servants of God." After his death on March 12, 604, Gregory was immediately canonized by popular acclamation. The title "the Great" was bestowed on him in the year 1298 by Pope Boniface VIII.

Prayer

Jesus,
I desire to serve you
    with all my heart, my soul, my strength, and my mind.
Let me not fear your call to greatness
    but transform me in your example of servanthood.
All I have and all I am
    I place at your command.

Connecting With Gregory the Great

Scattered among change-makers in our Christian tradition we find people who come from humble, unknown backgrounds; here we might find people of royal lineage. Likewise, there are saints who lived their lives unnoticed and unassuming; there are saints who were prominent in their time and influential in our own. It matters not which we are. What matters is if we are willing to let ourselves be used by God for the good of God's people and the glory of God's name. What matters is God.

Gregory knew this, and rather than shying away from his giftedness of family and talent, he actively placed all he had at God's disposal. His administrative ability saved the lives of many during the time of plague and inspired others to do the same. His strength of character and conviction reformed a Church that had lost self-discipline and public respect. And his creative originality sought new answers to problems rather than relying on the practices of the past.

Formed by the discipline of his monastic life, Gregory drew his moral and mystical teaching from Scripture. He embraced great and small with charity and possessed the humility to learn from his people. Before the term *servant leadership* came upon the business world, Pope Gregory used the description for himself while holding the most powerful position of his time.

Servant of the servants of God, you and I are called to be the same.

Reflect and Pray

✝ What gifts do you experience in your life today that you have received from your ancestors?

✝ How are you called to place your giftedness at the service of God and God's people in your own unique time and place?

✝ What reforms within Church and society cry out for your attention? Name one action you can take to address one of these situations.

Hilda of Whitby
(614–680)

Thou wast called mother by all who knew thee.

Five noted bishops trained at her school.

A stable boy became England's first Christian poet
at her dinner table.

Celtic Christianity gave way to Roman ways
at the synod over which she presided.

Mary Michael Kaliher, OSB

Hilda of Whitby (known in her time as Hild of Streonshalh) was born in 614, the daughter of Hereruc and Breguswith. Unlike many of the female mystics and monastics of the Middle Ages, Hilda left no journals, prayers, letters, or sermons as records of her amazing life. What little is known comes from *The Ecclesiastical History of the English People* by the Venerable Bede, who was born approximately eight years before her death.

Hilda lived during one of the most dynamic times of the English church. During this era, the main occupation for men was warring. Consequently, at the time of Hilda's birth, her parents were in exile, along with her grand-uncle Edwin of Deira. In 616 Edwin successfully united the kingdoms of Deira and Bernicia into the kingdom of Northumbria and became its king. When Hilda's father died, she and her family took up residence within the royal court. This arrangement afforded Hilda the education, privilege, and freedom of a daughter of nobility in the still largely Celtic society.

The Celtic peoples of Britain had heard the Gospel proclaimed by Saint Alban and others by the third century and had integrated it into their lives. However, in the 400s and 500s, a massive invasion of Germanic peoples forced the native Celts out of what is now England and into Wales, Ireland, and Scotland. Missionaries from the continent arrived on the heels of the invaders, bringing with them the influence of Rome. The Roman impact intensified at the end of the sixth century when Pope Gregory sent Augustine to establish an archdiocese of England and himself as the archbishop. Paulinus arrived in 601 to assist Augustine and labored tirelessly to convert the Celtic pagans to Roman Christianity.

Hilda, along with her older sister Hereswith and their mother, was part of the court when Paulinus successfully converted the king. As went the king, so went the entire people; thus Hilda was baptized in the river York on Easter day 627, along with the large household of the king. It seems likely that when King Edwin was killed in battle in 633, she went with Paulinus to take refuge in Kent. It also seems likely that she would have married and been widowed, without children. These are simply suggestions by historians, for little is known from the date of her baptism until the year 647.

The record of her life picks up again in that year, when at age thirty-three she prepared to join her sister at the monastery at Chelles, Gaul. Aidan, Bishop of Lindisfarne, asked her to remain in England and presented her with a parcel of land on which to form a new monastery according to the Celtic tradition. A year later he appointed her abbess of a monastery at Hartlepool, and in 657 Hilda became the founding abbess of another monastery at Whitby, then known as Streonshalh. She remained at Whitby until her death twenty-three years later.

Hilda's gifts of administration and leadership were remarkable. According to the tradition of Celtic monasticism, Hartlepool and Whitby were double monasteries (male and female), with members living in small houses of two or three and coming together for worship. As abbess, Hilda emphasized the common life and monastic discipline. She greatly emphasized education, especially the study of Scripture. All property and goods were held in common, and good works were to be undertaken by all; the virtues of justice, piety, chastity, peace, and charity being conscientiously observed.

The power and influence of abbesses was at its height during this time, for the monastic structure of the Church meant that abbesses were often considered comparable to a local bishop. Hilda of Whitby was considered a wise steward and thus received many donations of land and livestock. She was engaged in recruiting students and staff for her school, improving the land, constructing buildings, supervising farms and livestock, administering justice in the village, and caring for the spiritual well-being of the people in the surrounding areas. She was known to encourage and mentor others, never fearing to be outshone by her students intellectually or spiritually.

In matters of religious culture there was a meld in Hilda of the two traditions vying for supremacy in England at this time. Paulinus baptized her in the Roman tradition; however, Bishop Aidan practiced the Celtic, and it was he who greatly influenced her adult life. Hilda was held in high regard, as is evidenced by the fact that King Oswiu asked her to host the 664 Synod of Bishops. This was not a mere feeding and housing of those who participated in the synod; indeed, Hilda of Whitby was integrally included in the proceedings. The key questions at this synod related to differences between the Roman and Celtic traditions of Christianity; one particular example concerned a consensus on the date of Easter.

Hilda supported the Celtic view, but when the decision was made to adopt the standards of the Roman Church, she accepted it to advance the unity of the Church in England. The synod of Whitby not only changed the date for the celebration of Easter, but imposed a Roman diocesan organization on the essentially monastic structure of church over which Hilda had presided. It gradually meant the end of many of her progressive reforms that were mostly based on Celtic traditions, but still Abbess Hilda stood courageously as a reconciler and prudent leader.

Nine years after the synod, Hilda of Whitby contracted an illness that never left her. She lived the next seven years with a continuing commitment to all who came to her for guidance and a deep gratitude for all she had received from her God. She died on November 17, 680, at the age of sixty-six, considered at the time to be an advanced old age.

Prayer

> Jesus,
>> heal the chasm that has arisen
>> between people who disagree.
> Free the creative feminine
>> that seeks to nurture and reconcile.
> Stir up within us your Spirit,
>> your vision,
>> your very self.

Connecting With Hilda of Whitby

During World War II, a German widow hid Jewish refugees in her own home. As her friends discovered the situation, they became extremely alarmed. "You are risking your own well-being," they told her.

"I know that," she replied.

"Then why," they demanded, "do you persist in this foolishness?" Her answer was stark and to the point. "I am doing it," she said, "because the time is now and I am here."

During Hilda of Whitby's unique time and place, she was given a position of influence that impacted the next fifteen hundred years of Church history. She stood at the crossroads of two streams of Christian expression: the Celtic and Roman. In her day, women served as powerful leaders within the emerging Church and newly founded religious houses. But hers was also a time of war, upheaval, and chaos.

This was her time and her place.

We likewise stand today in a time and place that has formed who we are—individually, as a nation, as a church, as a world. We can point to examples of vast creativity and those of static routine. There have been times of dialogue and times of silence. People have engaged with one another across differences and have violently taken positions of polarity.

It can be tempting to look back on certain historical eras as "golden days," but who would decide which that would be? Though calling other eras *golden* is tempting, to do so is to gaze in a very shallow manner. When we do this we deny that there is only one moment in which we can make our response—and that is *now*. As disciples of Jesus we are always called to go beyond where we are now, but our *present* is the only starting place.

Abbess Hilda of Whitby was called "Mother" by all who knew her because she nurtured life in all its manifestations. She was able to be faithful to each moment as it presented itself because she knew that ultimately it was God who was faithful. It was God who called her, empowered her, and asked her to stand courageously in the midst of turmoil. Hilda responded by becoming deeply steeped in holy Scripture and engaging in acts of charity, and she encouraged others to do the same. She spoke truthfully, listened reverently, and *let go* of expectations for a particular outcome. She encourages us to do the same.

Reflect and Pray

- ✟ Hilda of Whitby opened her monastery to everyone, offering hospitality to travelers from nobility to local peasants alike in exchange for a song, a story, or whatever knowledge they could share. When have you been gifted as the recipient or provider of hospitality?

- ✟ Name some nurturing or mothering people in your life. Whom do you nurture/mother?

- ✟ What gifts and challenges are uniquely yours in your time and place? What do you hear yourself called to do?

Boniface
(680–754)

In her voyage across the ocean of this world,
the Church is like a great ship being pounded
by the waves of life's different stresses.
Our duty is not to abandon ship
but to keep her on course.

It happened on a bitter winter day in 723.

It happened in the area of Germany called Hesse, controlled by the fierce Chatti tribe, who had defeated the mighty Roman army more than once.

It happened at the sacred oak where animals and occasionally even humans were sacrificed to the thunder-god Thor.

It happened in the style of many an Old Testament prophet: the one true God met head to head with the local pagan god.

The Anglo-Saxon missionary Winfrid, later to be called Boniface, had arranged a meeting with the followers of Thor to prove that Jesus was the true God. He stripped to the waist, took an ax in hand, and stepped up to the sacred tree. The tribal leaders called on Thor to strike Boniface down with a thunderbolt; the Christians called on Jesus of Nazareth to protect him. At the moment Boniface raised his ax to strike the tree, a mighty wind sprang up, as if from nowhere. As the ax cut into the great oak, the tree was lifted up and split into four pieces by the wind, revealing itself to be rotted from within.

What they saw convinced all gathered to be converted to Jesus, and they were baptized into the Christian faith. Boniface took the wood of the tree and used it to build a Christian chapel upon that very place, dedicated to Saint Peter. It has been said that in the swing of that ax, German mythology met its death while the Christian faith was born. Boniface was the dramatic ax wielder.

Boniface, baptized Winfrid (which means "friend of peace"), had been born into a Christian family of noble rank in Devonshire, England. As a young boy, he listened spellbound to the monks who frequented his home. The fervor and vitality of the missionaries who had brought the Christian faith from Rome just two generations earlier were still alive. The missionaries' passion for spreading the faith by study and teaching caught his interest, and Winfrid resolved to enter the service of the Church.

Against his father's wishes, Winfrid studied at the Benedictine monastery of Adescancastre, near Exeter. After completing studies at the Abbey of Bursling in the Diocese of Winchester, he was appointed head of the school. Winfrid taught with such skill that notes from his classes were copied and circulated in other monasteries. At the age of thirty he was ordained a priest and added preaching to his teaching and administrative work.

Winfrid's intelligence and leadership virtually assured him a successful career in the English church, but Winfrid deeply felt the call to become a foreign missionary. Northern Europe and most of central Europe had heard the Gospel but needed catechetical instruction following their conversion. In the spring of 716, Winfrid and two companions set out with the intention of joining Saint Willibrord in Friesland, which then included the Netherlands and lands to the east. Their efforts were thwarted by the war being carried on between Charles Martel and Duke Radbod, hence they returned to England in autumn of that year.

In 718, Winfrid persistently set out again, leading him to visit Rome for the first time. While there, Pope Gregory II commissioned Winfrid and gave him the new name of Boniface (which means "does good"). Crossing back over the lower Alps, Boniface worked with Willibrord for three years, then continued his missionary vocation. Boniface returned to Hesse, evangelizing the pagans and reforming the clergy who had fallen into immoral or heretical practices. He baptized thousands, established churches, and founded monasteries; on November 30, 722, Boniface was elevated to bishop.

The famous incident of Thor's Oak in 723 refueled his crusade. Monks, nuns, and teachers came from England to help Boniface win over the pagan tribes. Monasteries were expanded and tribal leaders were converted. Pope Gregory III sent Boniface the ecclesiastical pallium stole in 731, appointing him archbishop of all Germany beyond the Rhine, with authority to found new bishoprics. Between 742 and 747, Boniface convened five Church councils, adopting strict regulations for the clergy, condemning local heretics, and infusing new zeal into the Frankish Church.

After these many years of administration, Boniface again felt the missionary vocation calling him. In his late seventies, he resigned as bishop, and with a band of fifty, he roamed the countryside, destroying pagan shrines, building churches, and baptizing masses of people. On the eve of Pentecost, 754, Boniface and his followers were attacked while encamped at Dorkum on the River Borne. The elderly saint was sitting in his tent reading as he awaited the arrival of a large group of new converts to be baptized. When the pagan looters attacked, Boniface commanded his followers to trust God and welcome the prospect of dying for their faith. His beaten body was carried to Fulda for burial, where it still remains. The book the bishop was reading is also at Fulda—dented with sword cuts and stained with the blood of the martyr.

Prayer

Jesus,
> let me live with courage and boldness
> in the eye of the storm,
> the cutting edge of mission territory,
> the total self-giving of martyrdom.

In whatever ways these appear in my day-to-day life,
> help me to stand confidently in you. Amen.

Connecting With Boniface

The years in which Boniface lived and worked were far from peaceful. Battles raged between the various Germanic tribes. Struggles for power were common both within the Church and among civil authorities. Poverty was widespread and education lacking. Into this tumultuous time came Boniface, offering the Christian faith as an alternative way of life. It reconciled tribal divisions and displaced local gods in favor of the one true God. And it countered the brutality of a war-centered culture with a vision of peace and kindness. This was the world and message of Winfrid (*friend of peace*), named Boniface (*one who does good*).

His methods were bold and dramatic. Boniface was restless, not for his own acclaim or ascent up the clerical career ladder, but because he knew people needed to be fed, healed, instructed, and converted to the Christian faith. Hindered by war, enticed by ecclesial promotions, and challenged by the infirmities of aging, Boniface endured all of these as temporary hurdles. And he shared his passion by traversing into unexplored fields to preach the Gospel of Jesus.

Boniface challenges us to live passionately and true to our own unique vocation. Some of us may engage in a way that is conventional and polite, others are experienced at the confrontational and controversial. Some men and women are called to organize, regulate, and administrate, while others, with the spirit of Boniface, need to keep moving to new frontiers.

We travel the ocean of this world together, each called to bring the different gifts we have been given. The course of our ship is driven by the dynamism of all interacting together; rocky at times, smooth at others. *All* are needed.

Reflect and Pray

✞ Over and over, Boniface returned to his original call to be a missionary to the heathens. Where do you continually find yourself returning? What are you longing to pursue? Write a letter to God and tell God about it and ask for help and courage.

✞ Winfrid means "friend of peace." Boniface means "one who does good." What does your name mean? What invitation do you hear in your name?

Charlemagne
(742–814)

To have another language is to possess a second soul.

The people of Italy were gathering. Pagan festivities recognizing the return of the sun intermingled with Christian religious services celebrating the birth of the Son of God. Day and night the villages were filled with song, prayer, and pageantry.

In Rome, a different scenario was taking place. Hidden in a corner, King Charles (*Charlemagne* in French) knelt in quiet prayer at the tomb of the Apostle Peter. In what has been called one of the best-known scenes of the Middle Ages, Pope Leo III went to him, laid his own hands upon his head, and crowned Charlemagne "Emperor of the Romans." All the people rose and cried out three times, *"Carolo, piisimo Augusto a Deo coronato, magno et pacifico Imperatori, vita et victoria!"* ("To Carolus Augustus crowned by God, mighty and pacific emperor, be life and victory!")

—*Christmas Day, 800*

Shutterstock: From "Historisk lasebok" published in 1882

The king who was at the center of this extraordinary event was born in the year 742 in what is modern-day Belgium. Charles was the namesake and grandson of the Frankish leader Charles Martel, who led Christians in victory over the Muslims in the famous Battle of Tours. It is from these two men that the great Carolingian dynasty took its name.

Educated by his mother, Bertrada of Laon, and the monks of St. Denis, Charlemagne developed a deep appreciation for the liberal arts and sciences. He learned to speak and read Latin as well as his native Germanic tongue, although he never mastered the art of writing. He cultivated the practices of his Catholic faith and developed a profound respect for the hierarchy of the Church, especially the pope.

Close to the throne of his father, Pippin the Short, Charlemagne mastered the art of military and political leadership. His physical stature naturally gained respect: he was tall and forceful in bearing. His speech was eloquent, and his intellect ingenious and astute. When Charlemagne gained the Frankish throne in 771, all of Europe quickly took notice of the charismatic king. As he rapidly conquered territory after territory, Charlemagne forcibly imposed conversion to the Roman Church upon the people, using violence if necessary.

This military approach to faith conversion revived the Roman Empire as the *Holy* Roman Empire. It also served as a precursor to the Crusades.

Still, the softer influence of his mother and the monks of his child-hood reemerged in Charlemagne's later life. He came to see that the pastoral ways of missionaries and bishops were more suitable than military conversions. Each cathedral and monastery was instructed by Charlemagne to set up a school, bringing in the learned from all over Europe. Girls were to be included in the study of literature and the arts. Schools of architecture and jurisprudence were established, liturgical and scriptural studies initiated. Charlemagne standardized Latin. He established the Rule of Benedict as the guide for monasteries, directed a revision of the Bible, and instituted changes to the liturgy.

Throughout his historic fifty-year reign, Charlemagne strove to bring to fruition the vision found in Augustine's *City of God*, with Church and state serving as aligned forces in the flourishing of society.

And he commissioned traveling bishops who were sent throughout the empire to ensure that the reforms of the papacy and the emperor were faithfully carried out. By the time of his death in 814, the Carolingian Renaissance had ushered in a slow reemergence of culture and learning in Western Europe, and the Roman Catholic Church was positioned as an ally and asset.

Prayer

Jesus,
    teach me to speak the language of love.
When I am tempted to use force
    let me show gentle strength.
When I desire revenge
    let me show forgiveness.
And when I seek my own glory
    let me remember your way of the cross.
Jesus,
    teach me to speak the language of love,
    for it is the language of you. Amen.

Connecting With Charlemagne

Canonized in 1165 by the antipope Paschal III and declared patron saint of France two centuries later, Charlemagne is no longer recognized as a saint by today's Church. However, his role as one of the most influential and contradictory figures in the history of Europe and the Church is beyond dispute.

Like Charlemagne, we are all a paradoxical bundle of rich potential. It is the work of a lifetime to disarm our tendency toward aggression and defensiveness. Charlemagne lived in a violent time, as do we. He viewed life as a series of battles he had to fight: for more land, for conversion to the Christian faith, and for triumph over poverty and illiteracy. This tendency to fight to achieve our goals, even if one is a warrior for a good cause, is within us all. It may be expedient and righteous; it is not, however, the way of Jesus.

The way of Jesus is to trust that violence never ceases by violence but by love alone. We can let the circumstances of our lives harden us and make us increasingly resentful and afraid, or we can let them soften our beings by making us kinder. Charlemagne softened. His conversion from violent warrior king to benevolent leader was not dramatic. It was more like the gradual maturing that happens in each of our lives, interrupting our destructive habits and awakening our hearts.

The essence of bravery is being without self-deception and seeing ourselves clearly. Charlemagne experienced the pain of losing half his children during his lifetime, for though he built an empire, only one of his sons lived to succeed him on the throne. He aged and lost his vigor, living the last several years of his life in immense pain and sickness. Despite his titles and triumphs, even despite his recognition by the papacy of the Holy Roman Catholic Church, Charlemagne suffered.

The language of triumphalism has no place in suffering nor in the speech of the ego. There is only the language of love.

Reflect and Pray

✝ What have been some of the greatest triumphs in your life as well as some of the most painful defeats? Where did you find God in each of these?

✝ Who speaks to you in the language of love? What do they say and how do they say it?

✝ When do you experience yourself speaking in the language of the conquering warrior? In the language of love?

Monks of Cluny
(founded in 909)

Monks should diligently cultivate silence at all times.

When the tenth century began, Europe was
at the midpoint of its darkest age. Charlemagne's
empire lay in ruins. The majority of people lived
in poverty while brutal nobility ruled over them.
There was no civil or religious figure to unite the
people; faith was superficial. Clergy were dishonest
and incompetent. War perpetual. The devastation
was so great that people truly believed the end
of the world was near. In fact, they sought it as a
release from the overwhelming suffering.

Shutterstock: History of the Church, circa 1880

It was into this dark hour, just nine years after the dawn of a new century, that a monastery was founded in the province of Burgundy, France. Its goal was the revival of the monastic spirit of sixth-century Benedict of Nursia. It would become one of the two major factors in revitalizing the Church and a key actor in the creation of the High Middle Ages.

Cluny was endowed by Duke William of Aquitane. He had murdered an individual in his youth and sought to make reparation by building a new monastery. It was not unusual for the rich nobility to repent this way, as it also assured that the benefactor and family would be included in the prayers of the monks forever. However, a variety of circumstances changed Cluny from being just one among many.

First, Cluny had the good fortune to be ruled by a succession of exceptionally able, holy, and long-lived abbots. Odo (927–942), Maieul (965–994), Odilio (994–1049), Hugh the Great (1049–1109), and Peter the Venerable (1122–1156) were friends and counselors of emperors, kings, dukes, and popes. These men had access to great wealth and influence with which to implement their reforms. They also had the wisdom and integrity with which to lead their many followers. And finally they were able to establish with full autonomy, free from interference by both the duke and bishop, as Cluny was accountable to the pope alone, and he lived in Rome.

Second, Cluny itself served as the authority over the many houses established in its name. This created a formidable network of influence. At its height in the middle of the eleventh century, the abbey had more than ten thousand monks and two thousand dependent priories throughout Europe. The Abbot of Cluny ruled supreme over monks who lived in France, Spain, Italy, and England. The customs and disciplines of the abby were followed in all the houses, while the privileges, high esteem, and independence from local bishops and secular lords that belonged to Cluny were likewise enjoyed.

The influence of Cluny was in the nature of a reform *movement* rather than simply a monastic house. Monasteries of the time had become lax and easy, where slumber had replaced study. Indulgence in food and drink had replaced fasting, and the acquisition of private wealth through "pay for pray" had become commonplace. Monastic silence had all but disappeared. Clerical abuse and disregard of celibacy were widespread, as was simony (the buying and selling of church offices). The monastery at Cluny challenged and then changed these abuses. It reestablished what was then felt to be the very *raison d'être* for monasticism, namely, prayer and intercession on behalf of the whole of society. In a feudal age of professional warriors, the monks of Cluny carried the distinction of being the professional *pray-ers*. And they did this with an enthusiasm that would be their shining achievement as well as their downfall.

The liturgies of Cluny were unprecedented in scale and grandeur. Their church was the largest church in Christendom, succeeded only centuries later by St. Peter's in Rome. The Liturgy of the Hours was embellished with solemn processions and elaborate antiphons. The numerous daily celebrations of Mass were accented with gold vessels, luxurious vestments, and a prominent emphasis on saints and relics. Feast days, such as the Commemoration of All Souls on November 2, were established at Cluny.

It could be calculated that a monk of Cluny spent at least eight hours in chapel on normal weekdays, excluding private prayer. Several other hours were spent in the preparation for the elaborate celebrations. Therefore, if one figures another eight hours for sleep, time for personal hygiene, and one or two hours for meals, little is left. Time for reading and the copying or illuminating of manuscripts was minimal, and in this monastic community, manual labor became almost nonexistent. Laborers were hired to carry on the work of the abbey as well as the traditional monastic works of charity and hospitality. And complicated systems were employed for keeping track of the hours of prayer, the donations received, and the prayers requested by benefactors.

Founded in 909 as a reform movement, Cluny itself was in need of reform two centuries later. Several external factors were at play: English and French nationalism created a climate hostile to monasteries ruled by someone in Burgundy. Plagues depleted the population of all Europe. New Orders such as the Cistercians were generating the next wave of ecclesial reform.

But the real demise of Cluny came from within as increasing prayers decreased their prayerfulness. A type of spiritual exhaustion set in when the external emphasis on pomp and ceremony, and distinction superseded inner conversion, while scrupulosity about personal perfection suffocated hospitality and care for the poor.

The monks of Cluny had in effect closed in upon themselves, and the abbey shut down in 1790.

Prayer

Jesus,
> I desire to serve you with all my heart,
> with all my soul, and with all my strength.
> Clear away all control that is not you.
> Help me to live with mindfulness and humility. Amen.

Connecting With the Monks of Cluny

The revival that was centered in the monastic life of Cluny impacted the entire European world and church in its day. At all times when a committed group of people live their ideals so intensely, their example elevates and generates life for all. Others begin to live more deeply and faithfully. And dreams of earlier days are rekindled; commitments to self-discipline and self-sacrifice are renewed and wonder, beauty, and awe encompass even the most trivial of activities.

However, the ever-present danger is one that eventually killed Cluny. That is the temptation to let activity, even though good and holy, to become an end in itself. It can happen in monastic life, as in the Church, our families, and our ministries. Ritual becomes ritualism and God an audience. Parents work so many hours to purchase "things" for their family that they have no energy to be present to one another. Agencies that care for the poor become complex bureaucracies with offices larger than their homeless shelters and more administrators than bed-makers. Completion of tasks overwhelms the reason for doing them, and efficiency prevails over creativity.

In every way and in every era of life, it is tempting to settle for the superficial. That is why the monk within each of us should diligently cultivate silence. We need to listen to the silence and remember that there is a God who is not us.

Reflect and Pray

- ✟ Cluny was a reform movement comprised of people who chose an alternative lifestyle. What choices do you see people making today that are countercultural? How do they challenge and inspire the broader community?

- ✟ Where do you find ritualism and perfectionism controlling your life? Ask God to help you return to the tender idealism with which you began.

- ✟ What practices do you incorporate in order that your life be more balanced? What role does silence play in your life?

Hildegard of Bingen
(1098–1179)

Viriditas

Viriditas

Ever green. Ever vital.

Viriditas is Hildegard.

Her fame is on the rise
  eight hundred years after her death.

Her music has risen to the top forty.

Her mandalas adorn computer screens,
  her medicinal practices intermingle
  with high tech,
  her writing is embraced by New Age
  and traditional religion.

Viriditas!

Sv.
Hilde
garda·

Hildegard was born in 1098 to Hildebert and Mathilda of Bermersheim, Germany, in the year Urban II announced the first Crusade. Religious fervor was high, and as their tenth child, Hildegard was tithed to God at birth. Even at the young age of three, Hildegard is reported to have had luminous visions, but she kept these secret due to their unusual nature. In 1106, at the age of eight, Hildegard was entrusted to the daughter of Count Stephen II of Sponheim, the anchoress Jutta. In an actual mock funeral ceremony, Hildegard received her last rites from the bishop and was proclaimed "dead to the world." She then lived in Jutta's castle with about a dozen other girls from noble families, where they learned reading, writing, Latin, music, and handiwork.

At age fourteen, Hildegard made vows as a Benedictine nun under Bishop Otto of Bamberg and entered the enclosure. She, like Jutta and the other nuns, lived alone in a simple cell attached to the church of Mt. St. Disibod Abbey. The cell had three windows: one window for food provided and refuse removed, a window for visitors who came for spiritual guidance and prayer, and a window to attend Mass and liturgy celebrated by the monks of St. Disibod.

Jutta was also a visionary and thus attracted many followers who came to visit her at the enclosure. Hildegard and Jutta most likely prayed, meditated, read Scriptures such as the psalter, and did some sort of handwork during the hours of the Divine Office. Nothing was written about the twenty-four years that Hildegard lived in the convent with Jutta, but it was undoubtedly a time of rich growth and learning. This might have been the time that Hildegard learned to play the ten-stringed psaltery and studied psalm notation. In all likelihood, she worked in the herbarium and infirmary of the convent, thus becoming acquainted with the healing powers involving tinctures, herbs, and precious stones.

When Jutta died in 1136, Hildegard was elected the abbess of this young Benedictine community and served in that role for the next forty-two years. She blended her gifts as religious mystic, writer, composer, playwright, healer, and botanist, with a growing ability as administrator and organizational leader.

A few years after assuming leadership, Hildegard broke away from the dominating male monastery of St. Disibodenberg with her community, taking it to Bingen and calling it after Saint Rupert. Hildegard created quite a stir by proposing not only to relocate her women to a new monastery, but to build one on a mountainside that stood alone and was not protected by a men's monastery or the dwelling of a bishop. She chose to take with her only a single monk as celebrant for the Mass: her friend, her scribe, her editor, and her confidant, Volmar.

During the first half of her life, Hildegard confided her visions only to Jutta and the monk Volmar. However in 1141, at the age of forty-two, Hildegard had a vision that transformed everything. She experienced a blinding light of exceptional brilliance that flowed through her entire being: her heart and breast aflame—not burning, but warming. In this encounter Hildegard understood God's call to write her visions and share them with the people of her time.

Her first and best-known work is entitled *Scivias*, that is, "Know the Way." In it she sums up, in thirty-five visions, the events of the history of salvation from the creation of the world to the end of time. *Liber Vitae Meritorum* ("Book of Life's Merits" or "Book of the Rewards of Life") and *Liber divinorum operum* ("Book of Divine Works," also known as *De operatione Dei*, "On God's Activity") followed.

In addition to her mystical experiences, Hildegard's prolific writings included mystery plays, an opera, and poems, as well as 345 letters to popes, emperors, and the common people. Their subject matter ranged from theology to natural history to healing. Hildegard even invented an alternative alphabet and new words with which to describe her experiences of God. The most famous of these is *Viriditas*—greening life-energy. In 1165, Hildegard founded a second monastery for her nuns at Eibingen. And from 1158–1171 she embarked on four major preaching journeys though she was past sixty years of age, for nothing could damper the fire within her.

One of her greatest challenges came toward the end of her life. As often happens for prophetic people, Hildegard was placed under an interdict by local ecclesial authorities. The interdict, which barred Communion and the singing of the Divine Office, was held upon her nuns for many months. During this time, Hildegard wrote a series of letters describing her experience of the role of music as a bridge uniting "this world" and the *world of all beauty and music.*

The interdict was lifted, but Hildegard had little time to enjoy it. She died only months later, on September 17, 1179. Hildegard was one of the first persons for whom the Roman canonization process was officially applied, and the process took so long that four attempts at canonization were not completed and Hildegard remained at the level of her beatification. Her name was nonetheless taken up in the Roman Martyrology at the end of the sixteenth century. On May 10, 2012, Pope Benedict XVI extended the liturgical cult of Saint Hildegard to the universal Church in a process known as "equivalent canonization," and on October 7, 2012, she was named a Doctor of the Church.

Prayer

Jesus,
  awaken in me your greening energy
  to seek you as Sophia (Wisdom),
  to know you in my Breath,
  to hear you within the Cosmic Symphony,
  to love you as you have first loved me. Amen.

Connecting With Hildegard

Viriditas is the lens whereby Hildegard sees all life of the cosmos sacramentally. It is greenness, the greening life-power of God. It is the animating life force within all creation, giving it life, moisture, and vitality. Greenness is the central, unifying image that Hildegard uses to harmoniously interconnect all levels of life: cosmic, human, and celestial life within a Triune God.

What does this mean for us? In the view of Hildegard, *viriditas* means everything: the challenge of every era is to nurture the greening of each stage of life. The role of leadership is to nurture life's greening power wherever it is found. The goal of medicine is to restore the original flourishing of all creation. The call of the human person is to be embraced by God, encompassed with wings unfurled, and carried above, below, and through the world.

Reflect and Pray

- ✞ What color is your living?
- ✞ What seeks new life and greening energy within you?
- ✞ Hildegard spent thirty years in ordinary, unremarkable living, but it prepared her for public, prophetic ministry. What daily practices prepare you for the challenges you will face?

Thomas Becket
(1118–1170)

Remember how the crown was attained by those whose suffering gave new radiance to their faith.

The 1960 Broadway play starred Laurence Olivier as Thomas Becket and Anthony Quinn as King Henry II.

The 1964 film paired Richard Burton and Peter O'Toole. It won an Academy Award and was nominated for ten others.

Almost fifty years later the film was re-released, using the finest of digital technology.

Despite great stars, numerous awards, and sophisticated cinematography, they can offer only a superficial portrayal of the transformation of a royal playboy into a powerful man of God.

Wikipedia: Miniature from an English psalter, circa 1250, Walters Art Gallery, Baltimore

Thomas Becket was born in London in 1118. His father, Gilbert, was a Norman knight who had settled in London and become a prosperous merchant. His mother, also of French descent, was renowned for her regal beauty. Thomas, for his part, was tall and handsome; he excelled in athletic competition as well as piety and devotion.

Becket was educated at the Merton Priory in Sussex and at the University of Paris. When he returned to England at the age of twenty-one, he was appointed a clerk to the sheriff's court. Three years later he was taken into the household of Theobald, the Norman Archbishop of Canterbury. Thomas quickly climbed the ecclesiastical ladder, befriending people of power and enjoying the benefits that came with the office. In 1162, King Henry II of England appointed Becket archbishop of Canterbury.

In medieval England, the Church was all powerful and Canterbury the seat of power. Fear of going to hell was vivid in people's minds; they were taught that only through the Catholic Church could they be saved. Excommunication meant certain damnation, and it could be levied upon anyone, even the king himself. Since the pope was far away in Rome, the archbishop of Canterbury virtually held control of the church of England. He and the king were considered equals and typically ruled together.

As chancellor, Thomas Becket lived in splendor. He was renowned for his luxurious wardrobe and spent his days on lavish entertainment, travel, and sport. As archbishop, he made a complete change, living a life of austerity and penance. He consumed only bread and water, giving his expensive food to the poor. He wandered through the cloister hallways, shedding tears for his past indulgences and spending hours in prayer. Most troubling of all to the king was that Thomas Becket, his former friend and coconspirator, endlessly sided with the Church over the Crown.

The archbishop and king were in constant conflict. This tension came to a head when the king demanded that Thomas agree to the Constitutions of Clarendon (1164) in which Henry reasserted the rights of the monarchy over the Church. Initially, Becket accepted this pronouncement but then changed his mind after consulting with the other bishops. Becket was banished to France and remained in exile for six years.

While in France, Pope Alexander III worked to bring reconciliation between the archbishop and king to restore peace to the Church in England. On December 1, 1170, Thomas Becket returned, electrifying all of England. While he had been gone, Henry had defied the rights of Canterbury and had his son crowned successor by the archbishop of York. At once Thomas Becket began excommunicating bishops who had gone against the Church and followed the king's commands. Henry, in a rage of fury, shouted out something to the effect of "will no one rid me of this troublesome priest?"

Four knights took the challenge as a serious request, and on December 29, 1170, they rode to Canterbury and confronted the archbishop during evening vespers. They brutally killed him, leaving his body strewn on the cathedral floor.

Immediately, the people of Canterbury tore off his clothing and dipped pieces in the archbishop's blood to bring to their homes. Miracles were reported. The site quickly became a place of pilgrimage. Henry II begged the pope for forgiveness and walked barefoot through the streets of Canterbury as penance. The king entered the cathedral, knelt in prayer, and kissed the spot where Thomas Becket, Archbishop of Canterbury, had died. He wearily laid his head upon the tomb of his friend while priests flogged his back and shoulders.

Prayer

Jesus,
    you know I have made mistakes and have failed.
You know I have stood firm and have been faithful.
You know all things, my Lord,
    and still you love me without limit.
Fill me with the radiance of knowing
    this simple, unfathomable truth.
Amen.

Connecting With Thomas Becket

The distance of centuries can almost anesthetize the pain and suffering involved in living the Christian life. Martyrdom can appear a swift and valiant exchange for eternal reward. However, the story of Thomas Becket and Henry II tells of suffering that is long-lasting and intimate. The first is personal suffering; the second, relational.

Becket's sleepless wandering in tears and Henry's barefoot pilgrimage through the streets of Canterbury paint a clear picture of what happens when one is brought face to face with his emptiness and sin. Gone is the security of being identified with the majority; gone is the lying and pretense with which we can silence our questioning hearts. It is shocking to realize that we have become caught up in the big and grandiose while life happens in the small and daily. It is an invitation to conversion.

Thomas Becket and King Henry were not only co-rulers, they were friends. One can only imagine the personal angst of Becket to decide to publicly oppose his friend or the pain of exile from home and loved ones this caused him. Likewise, picture Henry pierced to the heart when he learns his words brought about Becket's murder. Unfortunately, it often takes tragedy to bring us to the realization that our lives are held together by an extremely fragile web. We stand as sinners—each one of us—held together in the forgiving grace and love of God.

Reflect and Pray

✞ When have you needed to stand in opposition to someone you love because of your convictions? What did your banishment or exile feel like?

✞ Thomas Becket and Henry II both experienced times of conversion and change. When did you experience a personal call to conversion in some way? How has that invitation impacted your life today?

Gertrude the Great
(1256–1302)

At leisure for love

There is a quiet
    that speaks life:

Crinkle-eyed gaze of old lovers

Flickering candle in the room of one at prayer
    the sleep of the newborn
    the passing of the aged.

There is a quiet
    that speaks life

And it is there my heart has gone

Curled in your lap, Mother God,

At peace in your embrace.

Gertrude of Helfta, born on Epiphany in 1256, was entrusted at age five to the care of Abbess Gertrude of Hackeborn, who enrolled her in the cloister school of Helfta. Nothing at all is known of her family roots; her writings vaguely imply that she may have been an orphan. Her friendship with the Hackeborn sisters, Mechtilde and Abbess Gertrude, was a dynamic force in her intellectual and spiritual formation. As a scholar, she was soon noted for her insatiable desire for learning, study of the Scriptures and Church Fathers, and love of the literary classics.

In recounting her conversion at age twenty-five in 1281, Gertrude described herself as *a nun in name and appearance only* until her mystical encounter with the youthful Christ. Since this grace-filled crisis occurred during the Advent and Epiphany season of 1280–1281, it is highly probable this experience coincided with her consecration. Gertrude reached the requisite age of twenty-five for this liturgical rite in 1281, the same year as her conversion; and Epiphany was one of the days recommended in the Roman Pontifical for celebrating the consecration rite. This celebration of a triple anniversary may account for the intensity and love with which Gertrude celebrated Epiphany throughout her life. The conversion crisis marked a dramatic shift in Gertrude—the beginning of her transformation and mystical journey into the heart of Christ.

The societal, cultural, and monastic forces that impinged on the milieu of thirteenth-century Saxony influenced and shaped their spirituality. Founded in 1229, Helfta's first years were unusually difficult and unsettling. The baronial wars necessitated frequent moves to safer locations; the nuns experienced continuous insecurity, anxiety, and even pillaging of their monastery because of the civil and ecclesiastical strife that frequently engulfed Helfta. The Helfta monastery itself was unjustly placed under interdict, presumably because of unfair taxation of their revenue.

In spite of the turmoil, the forty-year reign of Abbess Gertrude of Hackeborn (1251–1291), its second abbess, was considered the "golden age of Helfta." Under her leadership, the Helfta scholars and mystics made this monastery a highly renowned feminine center of learning and culture. Their scholarship focused on a mastery of the Latin classics, schooling in the liberal arts, and a diligent study of Scripture. Abbess Gertrude left a deep imprint on the contemplative spirit at Helfta, and her influence was particularly significant on Gertrude, who lived under her guidance for thirty years.

Gertrude's spirituality is best characterized as a fusion of cenobitic monasticism (one that stresses community life) with the biblical, liturgical, and mystical. Her years of scriptural study and fidelity to *lectio divina* served as the wellspring of her Trinitarian and Incarnation-centered mysticism.

Liturgical celebrations served as the context for many of her visionary encounters with God, Christ, and the saints. In her writings, Gertrude frequently expresses concern that her mystical prayer harmonize with the liturgy and that it not interfere with the community's ritual in any way nor draw attention to herself. Her writings are filled with abundant metaphors in naming God and Christ, a veritable treasure of biblical imagery and liturgical symbols. And her exquisite style combines the poetic with rhythmic prose. The manuscripts of her exegetical works on the Scriptures are lost to us, but an outstanding characteristic of Gertrude was her *libertas cordis*, her freedom of heart. Gertrude interpreted her *libertas cordis* as a rite of passage from bondage to this freedom of heart—detachment from things and attachment to Christ through self-surrender in love. In it, she identified the chains that had fettered her in mediocrity and an inordinate love of the intellectual pursuit. Therefore, Gertrude's conversion crisis initiated an ongoing liberation process that transformed her from an infatuated scholar to an ardent God-seeker and God-lover. Modeling her contemplative style on John, the disciple whom Jesus loved, she was concerned with keeping her heart detached and free—free to be one with the entire cosmos and celestial choirs in jubilant praise of God.

Outwardly her life was that of a simple Benedictine nun living in the mutual support and challenges of community. The Helfta writings contain entries describing fatigue, illness, and daily manual labor such as laundry and cleaning, which were as much a reality in their community as the beauty of liturgy and passion for learning. Gertrude's boundless charity embraced rich and poor, learned and simple; it was manifested in tender sympathy toward the souls in purgatory and in a great yearning for the perfection of souls consecrated to God. Her humility was so profound that she wondered how the earth could support so sinful a creature as herself. Her raptures were frequent and could so absorb her faculties as to render her insensible to what passed around her. She therefore begged God, for the sake of others, that there might be no outward manifestations of the spiritual wonders with which her life was filled.

Though never formally canonized, the name of Gertrude was inscribed in the Roman Martyrology in 1677, and her feast was extended to the universal Church by Pope Clement XII. She is the only woman saint to be called "The Great."

Prayer

> Jesus,
>> to you I sing a hymn of love
>> through you I act and speak in love
>> with you I walk in charity and love
>> in you I seek to live. Amen.

Connect With Gertrude the Great

When we expect to touch or capture something beyond the limits of our ordinary reach and radius, we automatically extend our grasp by standing on tiptoe. Standing on tiptoe entails risk, or the possibility of not attaining our aims. It requires having a good sense of balance and equilibrium if attempted for any length of time. When children stand on tiptoe, they quickly begin to skip, for it is a joyful, liberating dance step.

Saint Gertrude, a late-thirteenth–century mystic, challenges us to stand on tiptoe of expectation and discern what new ventures may be within our reach in our own time. Her uniquely feminine approach to God calls us to reach for the expansiveness in God-naming and God-imagery revealed in holy Scripture. Through a profusion of imagery—scriptural, catholic, and lovingly bold—she shows us how to pray and minister to others in forms that transcend sexist, temporal, and spatial limits. Her contemplative vision, borne of seeing and loving with the heart of Christ, is the fruit of her love of learning and her ever-impelling yearning to see God face to face.

It has been said that what distinguishes Gertrude from other mystics is her conscious and joyous celebration of her womanhood in Christ. This inner liberation defied the gender constrictions of her time. And we are invited, male and female, to be free of the constrictions of ours. Maybe the invitation of all days is to let the prophetic Word of God form and free us; to not only be "alert" to the signs of the times but "aroused," as was Gertrude, by the God of passionate love to reach upward, outward, and deep within.

Reflect and Pray

✝ When and where do you take the leisure to be available to God's love?

✝ Write a love letter to God, expressing your dreams for the future, gratitude for the past, and inner experience of the present.

✝ The Bible has hundreds of images and names for God. Make a list of the ways you have addressed God over the years; what does this teach you about the nature of your relationship?

Fra Angelico
(1387–1455)

*Anyone who does Christ's work
must stay with Christ always.*

In the beginning.God created
  and there came forth light and life
  color and shape
  sound and silence.

In the beginning God created
  and there came forth man and woman
  a work of art in God's own image
  a masterpiece.

In the beginning God created
  and breathed forth his Spirit into humanity
  that they, too, may create.

Wikipedia: *The Annunciation* is located in St. Mark's Convent.
Wikipedia: Posthumous portrait of Fra Angelico by Luca Signorelli
(circa 1501)

Guido di Pietro was born around 1387 in Tuscany, near Florence, Italy. Nothing is known of his parents. As a young man, he and his brother Benedetto were trained as manuscript makers and illuminators. They took vows to become monks in the Order of Dominican Preachers in Fiesole. Completing their novitiate in 1408, they became full Dominican friars about 1418, and Guido was given the name Fra Giovanni da Fiesole. *Angelico,* "The Angelic," was a title bestowed upon him soon after his death as a way of honoring his work as an artist and servant of the poor.

Fra Angelico and Fra Benedetto operated a painter's workshop and a room for copying documents at the monastery in Fiesole. It was while at the monastery that many of Fra Angelico's early works were created and his style refined—a style described by Renaissance painter Vasari as painted by a saint or angel.

In 1436, Fra Angelico was one of several friars who transferred to the newly built Dominican friary of San Marco in Florence. This put him in the center of artistic activity of the region and brought about the patronage of one of the wealthiest and most powerful members of the city's Signoria, Cosimo de' Medici. At the urging of Cosimo, Fra Angelico set about decorating the new monastery with magnificent murals in the chapter house and common spaces, with intimate devotional frescoes depicting the life of Christ adorning the walls of each cell.

Freed from the constraints of wealthy private clients while at San Marco, Fra Angelico was able to artistically express his deep reverence for God and love of humanity. He painted none but sacred subjects with simple colors, humble characters, and fervent prayer. Fra Angelico never retouched or altered his work, believing that if the brush stroke had come from divine inspiration, it should thus remain. So passionate was his art that it is said he could not paint the crucifixion without weeping.

Fra Angelico's reputation was so celebrated that in 1445 he was invited to Rome by Pope Eugenius IV and there he was employed for the final years of his life, albeit a three-year hiatus to serve as prior of San Domenica at Fiesole. While at the Vatican, the artist was again confronted with the need to please his powerful patrons. He struggled to nurture the gentleness and humility that was at the core of his work with the lavish robes and jewels expected by his client. Fra Angelico was able to maintain this balance because his work emerged from his life centered in Christ. He stayed faithful to his monastic life, close to the poor, and grateful to the One who had given him the artistic gift.

Fra Angelico died in Rome in 1455, where he lies buried in the church of Santa Maria sopra Minerva. Pope John Paul II beatified him on October 3, 1982, and declared him patron of Catholic artists in 1984.

Prayer

Creator God, from you comes forth all life;
    stir within me your creative power.
Jesus, you are the incarnate God;
    unlock the beauty that lies deep within my soul.
Spirit, you are the mysterious Artist of the universe;
    breathe into my daily living the touch of the sacred. Amen.

Connect With Fra Angelico

Throughout the centuries, some saints have been known for their miraculous healings while others have started influential religious orders. Saints have ruled vast empires and have been prominent scholars and theologians. But Fra Angelico was none of these; he was a humble Dominican friar who painted. In doing so, Fra Angelico reminds us that the truth, goodness, and beauty of God cannot be confined to words. His sacred art invites us to enter into the mystery of God, who is intimate and yet utterly beyond. We as God's people are much richer for this!

In his 1999 *Letter to Artists*, Pope John Paul II encourages artists to believe that beauty is a key to mystery and a call to transcendence. The beauty they create, he says, can stir future generations to wonder, savor, and dream. This is the gift of Fra Angelico, popularized by the cherub faces that have made their way from corners of his frescoes to refrigerator magnets, note cards, and clothing of all sorts. He has offered to us the gift of wonder, that we may never take life for granted; as well as the gift of beauty, that we may gaze in stillness and allow mystery to be savored rather than analyzed.

At a time when few could read or write, sacred art was a primary form of catechesis. In our own modern time in which we are inundated with words and messages, sacred art invites us to enter into the deep silence from which all profound language arises.

Reflect and Pray

✝ Search out a picture of the work of Fra Angelico and gently sit with it. Ask God to speak to you through his sacred art. What do you hear?

✝ Walk through the day, seeing the world from God's delighted gaze upon creation. What do you see?

✝ Trust the Spirit of God to release creative power within you. Draw, paint, write a poem, sing or dance a hymn of praise. The Creator is inviting you to create.

Joan of Arc
(1412–1431)

In God's name, boldly march forward.

At age thirteen
  she heard the voice of the archangel Michael.

At age seventeen
  she held command of the military forces of a nation.

At age nineteen
  she was burned at the stake as a heretic.

Wikipedia: John Everett Millais

Joan of Arc lived a life of more passion, valor, and pain than most who have lived to be three or four times her age. This may be why she has served as the inspiration for numerous secular and religious plays, novels, poems, and films. She is inspiring us still.

Joan was born on January 6, 1412, to Jacques d'Arc and his wife, Isabelle, in the little village of Domremy, on the border of eastern France. At the time of her birth, a truce remained in effect between England and France, though internal strife within the French royal family greatly weakened that country's strength. One faction was led by Count Bernard VII of Armagnac and Duke Charles of Orleans. Their rivals were led by John the Fearless, Duke of Burgundy. The Burgundians would eventually capture Joan and hand her over to the English; a pro-Burgundian English bishop named Pierre Cauchon would later arrange her conviction on their behalf.

Joan's parents owned about fifty acres of land, and her father supplemented his farming work with a minor position as a village official, collecting taxes and heading the local watch. Situated in an isolated patch loyal to the French crown despite being surrounded by Burgundian lands, her home was the victim of several raids, and on one occasion her village was burned. It was while in the field keeping watch that Joan experienced the first of her visions. She described both verbal communication and figures that she could see and touch. Joan identified these visions as the archangel Michael, later joined by Catherine of Alexandria and Saint Margaret of Antioch, and on some occasions by hosts of saints and angels. Their message from God: save France by restoring the Dauphon (Charles, the heir apparent) to his rightful throne and driving the English enemy from the country.

Initially, Joan heard the saints' instruction to restore the throne through faithful prayer and pious acts. As the crisis grew, Joan heard the call to go to the local commander at Vaucouleurs to obtain an escort to take her to the royal court. In May of 1428, Joan arranged for a family relative to accompany her to see Sir Robert de Baudricourt, a vassal of the pro-Burgundian Duke of Lorraine, who had remained faithful to the Armagnacs. Baudricourt refused to see her, and Joan returned home.

Two months later, the villagers of Domremy fled the Burgundian army, and Baudricourt was forced to pledge neutrality. Orleans was placed under siege by an English army in October of that year, and Charles faced a desperate situation. Joan was finally granted permission to see Charles by correctly predicting yet another Armagnac defeat that would happen on February 12, 1429. Lord Baudricourt hastily arranged for an armed escort to bring Joan through enemy territory dressed as a man and presented the peasant girl to Charles.

Joan respectfully addressed herself to his royal majesty and informed him that she had been sent by God to assist him in battle. She convinced him of her legitimacy by telling him details of a prayer he had offered the previous year in which he begged God for help. Charles was elated, but first sent her to the city of Poitiers to be tested by a group of theologians as to her orthodoxy. Greatly impressed by her ability to hold her own before the strenuous examinations, the theologians granted their approval.

While still at Poitiers, Joan began dictating ultimatums to the English in which she declared that the King of heaven, Son of Mary, had pronounced Charles VII as rightful heir to the throne. She warned the English to return home or she would have to drive them out of France forcibly.

Joan was provided with a suit of armor and a banner with a picture of our Savior holding the world with two angels at the sides on a white background covered with gold fleur-de-lis. She established discipline in the troops and required church attendance and the sacrament of confession; Joan forbade swearing and she prohibited looting from conquered villages. As word spread that a saint had been sent to head the army, scores of volunteers came forward to serve.

Joan of Arc turned the tide of the war by breaking the English siege on Orleans. She inspired the French troops and managed a string of military victories through a series of small miracles that led to the crowning of the Dauphin as Charles VII, King of France, on July 17, 1429. She stood beside him at his coronation in Reims cathedral, thanking God for the victory. But she wearily confided that she was looking forward to returning home.

Joan of Arc had risen quickly to prominence, but her fate turned. On April 23, 1430, she was betrayed by someone within her own camp and was captured by Burgundian troops. Charles VII tried to save Joan in accord with the usual ransom, but the Burgundians refused, eventually selling her to the English. She was subjected to horrendous interrogation by the ecclesiastical court, who twisted her story to that of heresy and witchcraft since they could not execute her for beating them in war. Joan stayed true to her faith and purity of heart, to her belief in the voices she heard, and the military leadership she executed. But in the end, she was convicted for dressing in the clothing of a man.

On May 30, 1431, Joan was publicly burned at the stake. Eyes always on the cross, she continually proclaimed aloud the name of Jesus and invoked the saints. Her ashes were thrown into the Seine to thwart any attempts to honor her.

However, in 1455 an official ecclesiastical investigation found her innocent. She was canonized in 1920, although the Church hesitated to call her a martyr because it was at the hand of the Church that she was put to death.

Prayer

Jesus,
    help me to listen to your voice.
Teach me to trust your revelations
    embolden me to speak in your name
    release me from all that holds me back.
In your name, may I move forward boldly. Amen.

Reflect and Pray

In 1878 four Benedictine Sisters arrived in Dakota Territory to open St. Mary's Academy and Boarding School. Classes began the day after they arrived, with 21 boarders and 80 students crammed into three small classrooms. In 1885, seven more sisters arrived to begin the first hospital between St. Paul, Minnesota, and Seattle, Washington. They immediately began to care for the sick in an old hotel, charging one dollar per day of those who could afford it. St. Mary's Academy has grown into a university; the old hotel, into a major medical center. These sisters are just one example of the many women religious who moved forward boldly at a time when women were not even considered intelligent enough to vote. They are one example of women (and men) who have taken to heart the radical way walked by Saint Joan of Arc.

Joan of Arc serves as an example for all who listen to the voice of God and respond with strong faith. She defied the restrictions of her time, especially those placed on her because she was a woman. Joan teaches us that there are higher voices to which we must attend: the voices of our own angels, the voices of the poor and needy, the voices of the oppressed. Her story also lays bare the cost of radical disciple-ship and prophetic action.

Her deep mystical experiences did not result in comforting dia-logues with the Beloved; they led her to direct engagement in the events of human history and a commitment to action. Joan poured herself out, endured betrayal by those she served, and was executed by the Church she loved.

All by the age of nineteen.

Reflect and Pray

✞ Joan of Arc was willing to follow the voice of God even in the face of societal norms that told her it was not acceptable for her as a woman. Have you ever been held back because you were a woman, man, too young, too old?

✞ Write a letter to Joan, asking her to help you. Then, imagining what she would say to you, write a letter from her to yourself.

✞ Listen to the voice of your own inner angels inviting you to move forward boldly. If you knew you would not fail, what would you do?

Peter Claver
(1581–1654)

Slave of the enslaved…

It was said one could smell an approaching slave ship ten miles away, so horrific were its on-board conditions.

It was said every slave, whatever his size, was packed with only five feet six inches in length and sixteen inches in breadth to lie in.

It was said the men were chained together by their hands and feet, then fastened to the deck while they awaited purchase, which could take from six weeks to six months.

It was said one third of the slaves died while en route, and often they were considered the lucky ones.

It was said few dared defy the economic, political, and social dictates to help the slaves.

Peter Claver was one who did.

Peter Claver was born in Catalonia, Spain, in 1581. Bright and religious, he was destined for service in the Church and sent to the University of Barcelona. He graduated with distinction, and after receiving minor orders, he entered the Jesuit novitiate of Tarragona and was sent to Montesano College at Palma in Majorca for study. While at Majorca, Peter met the saintly Jesuit lay brother and college porter, Alphonsus Rodriguez. The humble Alfonzo served as an academic and spiritual mentor for Peter, setting him on fire for the exciting and active missionary life of the Jesuits.

After numerous requests to his superiors, Peter was allowed to leave Spain in April 1610 to become a missionary in the New World. It was a difficult journey, but he eventually landed in Cartagena, New Grenada, which is now Colombia. Peter completed his seminary studies and was ordained to the priesthood there in 1615.

The port city of Cartagena was strategically placed on the Caribbean Sea and served as a clearing-house for over 12,000 West African slaves a year. Jesuit Father Alphonse de Sandoval alone was ministering to the slaves, and Peter became his assistant. Though shy by nature, Peter immediately threw himself into organizing catechists, interpreters, and teams of volunteers to meet the slave ships. They brought food and clothing, medicine and kindness. They endured the stench that emanated from the pens where the people were herded with no hygienic facilities. And they preached the Good News and enfleshed the belief that all people—even these held captive—were precious in God's sight.

Father Peter Claver tirelessly baptized more than 300,000 African slaves in his 44 years of ministry. Perhaps even more significant, he considered them his parishioners, making regular pastoral visits, administering to them all of the sacraments, instructing them in the catechism, and caring for their spiritual and physical needs. In addition to caring for their needs, Peter Claver worked to change the attitudes of the slave masters and the laws that governed their lives. While he was not able to abolish slavery, he fought for laws that allowed for Christian marriage for slaves and that forbade the separation of families.

So successful was the charitable work of Father Peter Claver and his volunteers that the establishment became enraged. The white people believed that his congregation of unwashed Africans contaminated their churches. They resented his catechizing slaves and accused him of being erroneous for believing they were human beings. Many began to refuse the sacraments themselves, believing Claver was profaning the Blessed Sacrament by giving Communion to "animals."

An outcast among the wealthy and powerful, he became a much sought after minister among those who were considered worthless. He preached to the Moors and the Turks and recognized the Indian people as the beloved of God. And the most hardened and defiant would seek him out in the anonymity of the confessional, as it was said that not one criminal was put to death during his lifetime without the consoling presence of Father Peter.

In 1650, Father Peter Claver fell victim to the plague sweeping the city and was left partially paralyzed. His forty years of service to the slaves had left him weak and abandoned. For the last four years of his life, the only one to care for him was a former African slave. Upon his death on September 8, 1654, it was as if the people woke up and remembered. The civil authorities who had looked suspiciously upon his work to dignify the slaves and the Church authorities who had criticized his contamination of their sanctuaries now vied with each other to claim him as their own.

Peter Claver was buried with a lavish public funeral at the expense of the state, celebrated by the vicar general of the diocese. The Negroes and Indians also arranged for a funeral of their own, to which all the people were invited. He was canonized on January 15, 1888, by Pope Leo XIII in a double canonization with his mentor and friend, Alphonsus Rodriguez.

Named patron of those who minister with the black slaves throughout the world, Saint Peter Claver was never again forgotten.

Prayer

Jesus,

> free me from fear and prejudice
> lead me to those who are most in need
> challenge my compromised charity.
>
> Let me be totally poured out
> used up
> transformed by your Spirit.

Connecting With Peter Claver

Faye had worked with the banquet services of the local fraternal organization for years. She was kind, generous, and in her own down-to-earth way, intuitively aware of personalities. Upon meeting a new local CEO, she remarked, "He may shake my hand and say 'Nice to meet you,' but everything about him tells the truth. He's thinking *Isn't it nice for you to be able to meet me?*"

Peter Claver met people—at the ships, in the hospitals, in poverty, and at their deathbed. His greeting was always honest; it came through in his words, but even more so in his actions. His greeting said, "*You* are God's image and likeness. *You* are worthy of decent care. I am blessed to meet you."

In the long line of people who took seriously Jesus' command that we serve the least of his people, Peter washed the feet of the outcasts, kissed the wounds of the repulsive, and tenderly held the dying. In his consuming passion he challenges our self-proclaimed need for balance. In his kindness, he unsettles our tendencies to self-satisfaction. And in his final years, spent and forgotten, he exposes our desires for recognition and reward.

In each person he met, regardless of race or status, he met only Christ.

Reflect and Pray

✞ Recall a time when you have been greeted by someone and experienced yourself as truly important in his or her eyes, as a blessed child of God.

✞ Who are the enslaved and outcast among your local community? How can you respond to them?

Kateri Tekakwitha

(1656–1680)

"Jesus, I love you."

"Jesus, I love you." These were her last words as Blessed Kateri Tekakwitha died at the young age of twenty-four.

"Jesus, I love you." These words accompanied Kateri as she fled her village and walked more than two hundred miles to the Catholic mission near Montreal.

"Jesus, I love you." These words cost Kateri her family, her village, and ultimately her life.

Wikipedia: Father Chauchetière, circa 1690

Kateri Tekakwitha was born in 1656 in the Mohawk fortress of Ossernenon near present-day Auriesville, New York. Her father, Kenneronkwa, was a Mohawk chief who practiced traditional religious ways; her mother, Tagaskouita, had been baptized and educated by French missionaries. Tekakwitha's early life was filled with a rich integration of the two spiritualities.

When Tekakwitha was four, a smallpox outbreak ravaged the village, taking the lives of her parents and baby brother. It left Tekakwitha a vulnerable orphan—weak, scarred, and disfigured. It also left her partially blind, making it necessary for Tekakwitha to feel her way as she walked, especially when blinded by the bright sun. She was then adopted by her two aunts and her uncle, who was a chief of the Turtle clan.

Her new family discouraged any practice of the Christian religion, and so Tekakwitha's life took up the familiar rhythm of all young Native American girls. She learned to work in the fields, care for the home, collect water from the stream and berries from the woodlands. Despite her poor eyesight, Tekakwitha became skilled at beadwork and traded wisely with other villages. As the adopted daughter of a tribal chief, she was sought after as a politically valuable marriage partner.

All these activities placed Tekakwitha in the circle of friendship shared by the women of the village but left her feeling empty. Memories of her mother's devotions lingered in her mind. Stories of the Catholic faith continued to stimulate her imagination and animate her desire to live a life of holiness. Her escapes into the solitude of the woods increased her desire for intimacy with God. When her uncle took away the rosary that had been a gift from her beloved mother, Tekakwitha's determination to pursue the Christian faith only intensified.

On Easter Sunday, April 18, 1676, Tekakwitha was baptized by Father Jacques de Lamberville, a Jesuit missionary. She took the Christian name Kateri, which is Mohawk for Catherine and the patron saint Catherine of Siena. Because her newfound religious zeal was not accepted by the people of her village, she became an outcast. So when Kateri continued to hold strong to her faith, the hostility intensified and she received threats to her life.

In July 1677, Kateri fled to an established community of Native American Christians. Her journey to the Catholic mission of St. Francis Xavier at Sault St. Louis took more than two months and covered more than 200 miles. When she arrived at the community, Kateri immediately set herself to the care of the sick and poor. Though unable to read or write, Kateri taught prayers to the children, as her mother had done for her. She also fashioned crosses out of sticks and placed them throughout the woods. The life of Jesus and his followers, the passion and death of Jesus, the love of Jesus for her and for her people—thoughts of these mysteries completely filled the hours of her day. She spent much time in prayer before the Blessed Sacrament. And it was said that when she prayed, her face lost all its scars and was radiant with beauty.

On March 25, 1679, Kateri took a vow of chastity that she may remain totally devoted to Christ, her beloved spouse. She lived fully and generously for the next year, in spite of increasing poor health. Kateri died on April 17, 1680. Her final words were, "Jesus, I love you." Immediately after her death, Kateri's scars vanished and her face was totally transformed and beautiful. Her gravestone reads:

Kateri Tekakwitha
Onkweonweke Katsitsiio Teotsitsianekaron
The fairest flower that ever bloomed among the red men.

Prayer

Jesus, I love you.
I thank you for your great love for me.
In the softness of the air and the summit of the mountain
    I see your love.
In the rhythm of the season and the sacred journey of life
    I see your love.
In the scars of rejection and healing of compassion
    I see your love.
May I live that others may see your love in me.
Jesus, I love you.

Connect With Kateri Tekakwitha

The story of Kateri Tekakwitha is simple, ordinary, and unsophisticated. Her prayer may evoke memories of childhood religion classes and Bible songs; her life, however, is a call to love Jesus totally, regardless of the cost.

Blessed with the Native spirituality of her father and Christian faith of her mother, Kateri lived close to the earth. She knew that stewardship of the earth's resources was a sacred duty for all God's children; therefore we have a special responsibility toward one another and the rest of creation. She is the patroness of ecology, nature, and the environment and calls us to a sacramental view of the universe.

Kateri was a woman who knew that life as a follower of Jesus was radical and challenging. Her scars visible to all, Kateri walked the journey day by day, doing whatever was asked of her. She walked through the pain of illness and loss. She walked the loneliness of rejection and ridicule. She walked the surrender of her vow of virginity. Kateri walked the 200 miles that it took to reach a Christian community. And now she calls us to take up the cross and walk.

Finally, Kateri drew her strength and bravery from her life of prayer. It was only in faithful communion with her beloved that she was able to walk the lonely journey of her life. It was in hearing the Word of God proclaimed in sacrament and creation that she was able to teach the children. And it was through prayer that her scars were healed and her face glowed transcendentally.

Reflect and Pray

✢ Where in the outdoors do you go to meet God, your Creator? What do you hear while there?

✢ What scars have you received in the journey of life? How can you bring them to prayer and allow them to be transformed into beauty?

✢ Kateri made little crosses of sticks. Create your own symbol or ritual to say, "Jesus, I love you."

Felix Varela y Morales
(1788–1853)

The one who taught us how to think...

An exemplary member of both the Cuban and North American communities

An educator, philosopher, orator, legislator, author, social reformer, and patriot

A defender of liberty, human and civil rights, religious freedom, education for all, the betterment of women and children

An advocate for the poor, the homeless, the sick, minorities, and immigrants, always practicing charity to a heroic degree

These are some of the descriptors adorning the plaque at the Padre Felix Varela Foundation in Miami. Pope John Paul II visited his grave and encouraged the process for sainthood that had been approved by the Congregation for the Causes of Saints in 1985. On Easter Sunday 2012, this man—who would be the first Cuban-born saint—was raised to the status of "venerable." President Jimmy Carter named the *Christian Liberation Movement* in Cuba *Proyecto Varela*. In 1997 the United States Postal Service honored Varela as a social reformer by issuing a 32-cent commemorative stamp.

The accolades of this man are varied: varied disciplines, varied nations, varied contributions. The unchanging core of Varela's life, however, was his untiring commitment to a transformation of society flowing from the Gospel of Jesus Christ.

Felix Varela y Morales was born in Havana, Cuba, on November 20, 1788. At the time, Spain controlled not only Cuba but the entire West Indian islands and much of Central and South America, Louisiana, and Florida. In 1794 his mother died. Since his father was frequently away serving as a captain in the Spanish Army, Felix traveled with his aunt to live in Saint Augustine, Florida, which at that time belonged to Spain. After the death of his father, Felix returned to Havana to enter the College Seminary of St. Charles and Ambrose. He was ordained on December 2, 1811.

Joining the seminary faculty within a year of his ordination, he taught philosophy, physics, and chemistry. By winning a scholastic competition, Father Felix obtained the first Chair of Constitutions established at the College of San Carlos. That position offered him a public platform on which to reflect on the ways to build a just society and develop a core of devoted disciples among his students. He was an educator who challenged his students to think, to question, and to dedicate themselves to building a more just society. Varela was convinced that it was not law that saved people, but personal virtue and public engagement activity.

Unfortunately, Varela's term at the college was short-lived, for in 1821 he was elected as a Cuban representative to the Parliament of Madrid. In his three years of service, Felix championed the abolition of slavery in Cuba and the independence of Latin America from Spain. Due to his continuing commitment to human rights, Varela was among those branded as political traitors and sentenced to death. Before he could be arrested, however, Varela escaped to the United States where he lived for the next thirty years, first as a political exile, then as a pastor and, finally, as Vicar General of the newly created Diocese of New York.

In New York, Father Varela continued to integrate his academic pursuits with direct ministry to the poor. He built churches and schools, and created social services for the mass of immigrants coming from Ireland and other parts of Europe. He created asylums for the sick during the 1830 cholera epidemic, and he ministered not from the safety of the rectory, but in the midst of the suffering. It was from here that he also continued to write.

Varela founded the first Spanish-language newspaper in the United States, publishing many articles about human rights, religious tolerance, and the importance of education. In 1824, Father Varela published *El Habanero*, which was a short-lived but bristling magazine regularly smuggled into Cuba. His themes remained consistent: the hollow bravery of words over deeds, the betrayal of the common people by the powerful, the call for a free Cuba. In one issue of *El Habanero*, he ascribes to "Independiente" (Love of Independence) what might be more appropriately ascribed to himself: "If you call revolutionary all those who work to change an order of things contrary to the welfare of the people, then I glory to count myself among those revolutionaries."

Prayer

Jesus,
>   sharpen my mind that I may think clearly
>   free my tongue that I may speak prophetically
>   soften my heart that I may feel compassionately
>   focus my vision that I may know your will.

Connect With Felix Varela y Morales

Martin Luther King, Jr., was fond of saying that most people, and Christians in particular, are thermometers that record the temperature of majority opinion rather than thermostats that transform it. Father Felix Varela certainly would have agreed with this indictment and committed his life to the formation of people who would take seriously their responsibility to be intelligent prophets.

Our efforts fail when they are based on pity rather than on compassion and solidarity. Our words betray when they are not matched with actions. This is the message Varela lived—that we are to live in a manner that brings together head and heart, intelligence and goodness. We are to care for the poor and to ask why they are poor; to speak against war and to alleviate the situations that cause conflicts to erupt. We are to allow the light of Jesus to reveal the stale conformity in our own lives and in the life of the society in which we have become comfortable.

To live like this may lead to exile as with Varela. It could lead to assassination as with King, or crucifixion as with Jesus.

We also know it is the way to resurrection.

Reflect and Pray

☩ Name a modern-day prophet who inspires you. What invitation do you hear for your own life through his or her example?

☩ Where do you believe you are called to be a prophetic presence: at work, family, church, or some other place? What message do you wish to speak?

Benedicta Riepp

(1825–1862)

"I saw a large tree growing up,
covered all over with beautiful white blossoms."

Adapted (by Owen Lindblad, OSB) from the
words of Mother Augustina Weihermuller, OSB,
of Eichstätt, on February 11, 1957.

She died young—having traveled from Germany
to Pennsylvania to Minnesota.

She died young—having founded six independent
communities of Benedictine sisters.

She died young—having spent her life for her
dream.

Mary Michael Kaliher, OSB

Benedicta Riepp was born June 28, 1825, in Waal, Swabia, Bavaria, to John and Katharina Mary Riepp. Baptized Maria Sybilla, her father was the town glassblower; her three sisters were named Johanna, Sophia, and Juliana. We know little more than this about her family.

Benedicta entered Saint Walburg Abbey in Eichstätt, Bavaria, in 1844 at the age of eighteen, making her first profession July 9, 1846, and perpetual solemn vows July 9, 1849. Saint Walburg Abbey had been founded in 1035 and named in honor of Saint Walburga, the great Benedictine missionary to Germany. The abbey had been closed by Napoleon's Secularization Act of 1806 and the nuns sent back to their homes. Several of the older nuns were allowed to remain at the abbey. Therefore, when Ludwig I restored the abbey in 1835, this elderly remnant immediately went about the business of recruiting and training new members.

Entering just eight years after the restoration, Benedicta was part of this time of refounding with all of its accompanying tension and enthusiasm. The community was small in number and poor, with tension between the elderly who had suffered immensely through the suppression and the young who were full of new ideas and new energy. Benedicta was certainly of the latter. Shortly after her profession, Benedicta was appointed novice mistress (a position traditionally reserved for a sister wise and experienced in the religious life) in addition to her teaching duties at the school. Three years later, at the age of twenty-seven, she volunteered to serve in the foreign mission of the United States, teaching the children of German immigrants who had settled near St. Marys, Pennsylvania.

Benedicta was named the superior. She was accompanied by Walburga Dietrich (age forty-eight), a choir nun, and Maura Fleiger (age thirty), a lay sister. After a difficult trip on the *Washington,* they arrived at the harbor in New York on July 3, 1852, and the three sisters came ashore on July 4. Greeted by the explosion of fireworks but not by the promised hosts to accompany them in this foreign land, the sisters made their way to St. Vincent's Abby, Latrobe, Pennsylvania, five days later. Their arrival was a surprise not only to the monks of St. Vincent's but also to the Bishop of Pittsburgh, whom Boniface had failed to inform. Nonetheless, after a short stay at St. Vincent's to procure the appropriate documents, the sisters moved onward to St. Marys, Pennsylvania. They arrived on July 22, 1852, and by fall, they opened a school for girls, receiving a combined salary of $25 per month.

In her role as superior of the new community, Benedicta engaged in extensive letter-writing, sending reports to Europe and appealing for financial help wherever possible. Her recurring themes expressed concern over the extreme poverty of immigrant students and families, as well as their own dire conditions. Benedicta described watching the children coming to school, half-dressed and almost numb from the cold, with nothing to eat the whole day except a piece of black bread. She wrote of the orphans they had taken into their already-crowded home and the challenge this placed on attempts to live the daily religious schedule of prayer, work, and community life. She expressed gratitude for the many young women who were coming to join them as candidates but was concerned because there was no convent for them to live out their religious life.

The rapidly increasing community reached a total membership of forty sisters by the close of 1855; fourteen had come from the motherhouse in Eichstätt, and twenty-six from the surrounding area. The average age was twenty-four. With so much energy and youth, Benedicta Riepp continued to reflect on her vision of new blossoms, growing where there was need, but she was undoubtedly amazed at how God was leading. Between June of 1856 and December of 1859, twenty women would branch out and found four new houses—in Erie, Pennsylvania; Newark, New Jersey; St. Cloud, Minnesota; and Covington, Kentucky.

All was not smooth, missionary zeal notwithstanding. Abbot Boniface Wimmer petitioned to have the new community separated from St. Walburg's Abbey, with the rationale that he knew best what was needed by the sisters in the United States. In Germany, St. Walburg's was an autonomous abbey of women, with the local ordinary having jurisdiction over their enclosure. Benedicta and the sisters seemed to expect the same relationship in the U.S., while Boniface considered himself the head of the women's community. He accepted new members without consulting Mother Benedicta or the community chapter, and he redirected funds sent to the nuns and used it for various construction projects for the monks.

Mother Benedicta Riepp stood up to the Abbot with prophetic vision and undaunted faith, causing years of tension. She responded to a request for sisters in Erie, Pennsylvania, establishing a foundation there in 1856 without his permission. In 1857, Mother Benedicta established a new foundation in St. Cloud, Minnesota, again enduring the protests of Abbot Boniface Wimmer. She traveled to Rome to plead their cause with the Vatican and returned with a decree that gave approval to the new convents, but Wimmer sought to have her banished from her convents and sent back to Germany. The bishops of Erie and St. Cloud intervened, however, allowing her to return to Minnesota and live there the rest of her life.

Mother Benedicta Riepp died from tuberculosis on March 16, 1862, at the age of thirty-seven. At the time of her death, Benedictine women were well established in the United States, and six independent communities were thriving. There are now more than forty monasteries in North America, the Caribbean, Taiwan, and Japan that trace their roots to her. They are her beautiful white blossoms.

Prayer

> Jesus,
>   kindle within me a pioneer heart.
> Strengthen my conviction,
>   encourage my fidelity,
>   set free my creativity,
>   and use me for your purpose.

Connecting With Benedicta Riepp

The story of Benedicta Riepp and her companions is a story that reverberated throughout nineteenth-century America. Catholic nuns enduring extreme hardship to establish missions managed to set up classrooms, open hospitals, and bring a Catholic presence to the frontier. More often than not, they also had to face exploitation and disdain by the very clergy who had requested their services. Often their community leadership would be removed if they proved to be strong or independent in thinking and replaced by someone who behaved more "appropriately" for a woman. Like Mother Benedicta Riepp, they proved themselves resilient, creative, and faithful.

In our time and place, we must be just as prophetic and passionate. New challenges face us as the Church struggles to proclaim the Good News of Jesus Christ in a technological, materialistic society. New immigrants are stretching our resources and hospitality, just as many of our own ancestors had at the time of Benedicta. New tensions about the role of women, the enculturation of worship, and the abuse of power are arising.

It may be tempting to flee or create a safe enclosure in which to pursue a private spirituality, but Mother Benedicta Riepp invites us to something different. We are called to witness a "staying power" that is deeply rooted in fidelity to prayer, centrality to mission, and a prophetic lifestyle. We have inherited a vision and a pioneering spirit gifted to us by those who have gone before. We have been asked to dream of a better future for all God's people.

Reflect and Pray

- ✣ Benedicta Riepp died young—having spent her life for her dream. How will we respond to her witness?

- ✣ For Benedicta Riepp, the blossoming tree was the image of her dream. What image do you have for your own life and mission? If you don't have one, ask God to give you one now.

- ✣ Reflect on a time that you have moved forward although other people and circumstances were not supportive. What did you learn about yourself through this experience?

Pope John XXIII
(1881–1963)

Aggiornamento!

Unprecedented population growth
Collapse of European Communist regimes
Rise of China and India as economic powers
Ongoing strife in the Middle East
Racial riots in the United States
A smiling grandfather as the leader of the
    oldest and largest organization in the world

Aggiornamento!

Let the Church be brought up to date.

Angelo Roncalli was born into a sharecropper family near Bergamo, in the foothill of the Alps, on November 25, 1881. He was fourth in a vibrant, faith-filled family of thirteen.

Angelo entered the Bergamo seminary at the age of eleven, where he began spiritual disciplines that would last his lifetime: making spiritual notes in a journal, the regular practice of spiritual direction, prolonged periods of prayer, and a commitment to the spirituality of Saint Francis as a member of the Secular Franciscan Order.

He studied at the Pontifical Seminary in Rome and was ordained a priest on August 10, 1904. Roncalli returned home to become secretary to the new and socially radical Bishop of Bergamo, Giacomo Maria Radini Tedeschi. The bishop was under investigation during the campaign against modernism of Pius X, and for a time Roncalli himself was also a suspect. When Bishop Radini Tedeschi died in 1914, Father Angelo continued to teach in the seminary and engage in many of the pastoral works the bishop had begun. When Italy went to war in 1915, he was drafted and did front-line service as a medic and chaplain.

When World War I ended, he returned to the seminary as spiritual director, but was called away again in 1921 when Pope Benedict XV appointed him the Italian president of the Society for the Propagation of the Faith. Father Angelo Roncalli was named Apostolic Visitor in Bulgaria and ordained bishop on March 19, 1925, taking for his episcopal motto *Oboedientia et Pax*. Thus began his twenty-five years as a papal diplomat for Bulgaria, Turkey, and France. Serving during World War II, he helped refugees from Nazi Germany by arranging "travel visas" from the Apostolic Delegation. He facilitated communication between prisoners of war and their families and dissuaded President Charles de Gaulle from banishing French bishops who had collaborated with the Nazi regime during the war.

Even in the most complicated political situations, Bishop Roncalli strove for Gospel simplicity, trust in the good intentions of the other, and trust in the grace of God. He endured the misunderstandings that arise when a person is ministering to those on the fringes of society; he withstood the criticisms of his collaborative style, especially respectfully working with the Orthodox and Islam.

In 1953 he was named a cardinal and sent to Venice, where he believed he would live out the rest of his days. Cardinal Roncalli continued to have special solicitude for the poor and joy in the pastoral duties of his vocation. However, upon the death of Pius XII, he was elected Pope on October 28, 1958, taking the name John XXIII. At the age of seventy-seven, Angelo Roncalli was at first viewed as a nominal force, giving the Church a few years of rest after decades of two world wars, the Great Depression, and rampant secularization.

Amazingly, within months of his election, John XXIII announced his intention to call a worldwide council in which to update the Church and address the spiritual needs of the present day. It was the first council since 1870, and whereas previous councils were typically convened to correct some doctrinal error, John XXIII called for a council in which participants looked at the contemporary world with the eyes of hope, mercy, and faith. He went so far as to call the Second Vatican Council a "new Pentecost" and an invitation to open the windows and breathe fresh air.

Preparations commenced for this enormous undertaking of approximately 2,300 cardinals, archbishops, and bishops from around the world, accompanied by a small army of theological advisers and invited guests. October 11, 1962, was fixed as the opening day. On September 23, an x-ray revealed that John XXIII suffered from an advanced case of stomach cancer. It was to claim his life less than a year later, but not before he set into motion an event that unquestionably changed the trajectory of the Roman Catholic Church in ways that are still hotly debated today.

Prayer

Jesus,
>
> open my heart to the Spirit's prompting
> free me from the staleness of habit and routine
> enkindle within me the fire of creativity
> send me forth as your servant
> teach me to gift the world with a smile.

Amen.

Connecting With Pope John XXIII

Aggiornamento!

It seems likely that Vatican II will be known in history as the *aggiornamento council*. This phrase is the commission the council received when convened by John XXIII. Aggiornamento means "a bringing up to date." It was necessary for the Church. It is necessary for each one of us too. Blessed Pope John XXIII can teach us how.

Throughout his life, Pope John XXIII always remembered that he was Angelo Roncalli, the son of sharecroppers. It was from his family that he was nurtured in the faith; from his family that he learned the value of working together, the importance of dialogue and care for the poor. He helped reunite war-torn families because he knew the value of those connections. Likewise, he sought to unite a fractured Christian family by his ecumenical efforts because he knew Jesus' prayer that we all be one.

His episcopal motto, *Oboedientia et Pax*, carried him throughout life. Obedience and peace became his goal. The obedience of John XXIII was not unthinking acquiescence to an outer authority; it was the obedience that comes from deep listening to God. There is no quick and easy way to this kind of obedience. It takes years of faithful practice in prayer, spiritual direction, sacred reading, and humble living. It yields peace within the heart of one who has ears attuned to God, speaking even in the midst of strife.

The smiling Pope who is often pictured with his arms open to embrace the world invites us to live likewise. We are called to a conversion that brings us up to date with God's will for each of our lives today, in this space and time that is ours. Blessed Pope John XXIII was in love with life because he knew that he and all people were God's beloved.

Knowing this so profoundly, how can anyone fail to smile?

Reflect and Pray

✞ What do you remember or have you heard about Pope John XXIII? Ask some people who lived during the Second Vatican Council what they remember about him.

✞ Where in your spiritual life do you hear the call to renewal?

✞ What practices help you grow as a spiritual person? What practices do you need to become more faithful about?

Let Go

This Is Your Century
and—as Always—God's

While hiking in the mountains, a young woman slipped and fell from a cliff. As she was falling, she grasped a tree root and hung on for dear life. Over and over she cried out, "Help, is anyone out there?" but received no answer. Finally, she heard a gentle voice and realized it was God.

The young woman cried out, "God, I'm in real trouble here. Please help me. I'll do anything you want."

God calmly answered, "Let go of the branch."

After a moment of thought (and looking at the long drop to the ground), the woman loudly tried again, "Is anyone else out there?"

This popular story is often left here. But I wonder, *What if?* What if the woman had looked to her left and found people clinging to a tree root? What if she had looked to her right and found others in a similar situation:

> Mary of Magdala letting go at the tomb.
> Brigid of Ireland letting go in the fifth century.
> Thomas Becket of England letting go in the twelfth century.
> Peter Claver of Spain letting go in the seventeenth century.
> The local football coach, parish youth minister, or CEO of her place of employment letting go in the twenty-first century.

What if she had seen others hearing God's invitation and letting go, one by one? Their witness would have helped her follow the voice she heard, take the risk to "let go," and allow herself to trust God. Everything within her may cry out, "Is anyone else out there?" And she discovers that, yes, there is. They are her brothers and sisters in the communion of saints. I hope in reading this book you have discovered some kindred men and women from our two-thousand–year Christian history who have let go too. In the discovery, let yourself be inspired.

They have lived exciting and worthwhile lives, and you are invited to do the same. The men and women presented in this book sometimes dropped through the void of messiness and conflict. They experienced the fear of stepping out and risked seeming like a fool. They experienced disappointment in themselves, in their leaders, and even in their closest friends. If we are to answer the call in our century, we likewise will need to let go of all that holds us back and trust that God will be there to catch us. Twenty-one centuries of faith teaches us that it is God's faithfulness, not ours, that really matters.

We try and try to flatten out all the rough spots and imperfections into a smooth ride, but that is not the journey of Jesus whom we profess to follow. Rather, let yourself be drawn to discover what's waiting out there without yet knowing if you have the courage to face it. Let yourself be consumed by passion and zeal for God's house—this entire universe—without knowing how people will respond to your actions:

> Hilda letting go at the Synod of Whitby.
> Joan of Arc letting go at the stake in Rouen, France.
> Felix Varela letting go among the Cuban refugees.

They remind us not to compromise this one brief life we've been given. Now is our moment. This is our time to

> Listen to God's voice
> Stay close to the poor
> Release all to which we cling
> Let go and drop into the arms of our God.

Let Go
This is your century
and, as always, God's.

Prayer

Write a simple prayer, asking Jesus to lead you.

Reflect and Pray

✝ Reflectively speak the names of the twenty people included in this book. What comes to mind when you think about them? What is evoked within you?

Mary Magdalene (Apostle of Apostles)

Ignatius of Antioch (50–107)

Origen (185–254)

Macrina the Younger (327–379)

Brigid of Ireland (450–525)

Gregory the Great (540–604)

Hilda of Whitby (614–680)

Boniface (680–754)

Charlemagne (742–814)

Monks of Cluny (founded 909)

Hildegard of Bingen (1098–1179)

Thomas Becket (1118–1170)

Gertrude the Great (1256–1302)

Fra Angelico (1395–1455)

Joan of Arc (1412–1431)

Peter Claver (1581–1654)

Kateri Tekakwitha (1656–1680)

Felix Varela (Cuba) (1788–1853)

Benedicta Riepp (1825–1862)

Pope John XXlll (1881–1963)

✝ What are some of the gifts and qualities that have been with you since childhood? What gifts have others mirrored back to you in phrases such as "You are so creative" or "I like the way you speak about your faith"? What is the new edge of growth you are invited to take to use these gifts for God?

Bibliography

I have made every effort to give credit to sources that I used and to offer suggestions for other sources a reader may want to explore. However, many stories of the saints have been handed down over the years through oral tradition and local devotion. The origin may remain a mystery. But then again, isn't that the reality of all our lives?

Bede, The Venerable. *The Ecclesiastical History of the English People.* Edited by D. H. Farmer and R. E. Latham. New York: Penguin, 1991.

Bausch, William J. *An Anthology of Saints: Official, Unofficial, and Should-Be Saints.* New London, CT: Twenty-third Publications, 2012.

Bunson, Margaret R. *Kateri Tekakwitha, Mystic of the Wilderness.* Our Sunday Visitor, 1992.

Cahill, Thomas. *How the Irish Saved Civilization.* New York: Anchor Books, 1996.

Duffy, Eamon. *Saints and Sinners: A History of the Popes;* Third Edition. New Haven: Yale University Press, 2006. This resource is also available in a fascinating six-volume video series by Acorn Press.

Dwyer, John C. *Church History: Twenty Centuries of Catholic Christianity; First Edition.* New York: Paulist Press, *1985.*

Ellsberg, Robert. *All Saints: Daily Reflections on Saints, Prophets, and Witnesses for Our Time.* New York: The Crossroad Publishing Company. 1997.

Eusebius: The Church History. Translated by Paul L. Maier. Grand Rapids: Kregel Academic and Professional, 2007.

Galli, Mark, and Olsen, Ted, editors. *131 Christians Everyone Should Know*. Nashville, TN: B&H Publishing Group, 2000.

Knowles, David. *The English Mystical Tradition*. New York: Harper Torchbooks, 1961.

The Rule of St. Benedict. Edited by Timothy Fry. New York: Vintage, 1998.

Ghezzi, Bert. *The Voices of the Saints. A Year of Readings*. New York: Image/Doubleday, 2002.

Hollermann, Ephrem. *The Reshaping of a Tradition: American Benedictine Women, 1852–1881*. St. Joseph, MN: Sisters of St. Benedict, 1994.

The Liturgy of the Hours. International Commission on English in the Liturgy Corporation, 1974.

Martin, James. *My Life With the Saints*. Chicago: Loyola Press, 2007.

New Catholic Encyclopedia. 15 volumes. 2nd ed. Detroit: Gale, 2002.

Noll, Mark A. *Turning Points: Decisive Moments in the History of Christianity*. Grand Rapids, MI: Baker Academic, 2012.

Pelikan, Jaroslav. *The Christian Tradition*. Chicago: University of Chicago Press, 1975. A five-volume set that traces the development of Christian doctrine from the first century to the twentieth.

Schmitt, Miriam, and Kulzer, Linda, editors. *Medieval Women Monastics. Wisdom's Wellsprings*. Collegeville, MN: Liturgical Press. 1996.

Schmitt, Miriam. Unpublished research and manuscripts about the medieval women monastics held in the archives of the Annunciation Monastery, Bismarck, ND.

Series for Research and Reflection

An Hour With… Liguori, MO: Liguori Publications. This series contains a number of pamphlets that offer an opportunity for reflection and prayer with the wisdom of a saint or religious leader.

Butler's Lives of the Saints. ed. Thurston, Herbert, and Atwater, Donald. London: Burns & Oats, Ltd. 1956. First written in the mid-eighteenth century, this four-volume set was revised in 1956 to include 2,565 saints compared to the original 1,486.

Companions for the Journey. Winona, MN: Saint Mary's Press. This series contains 22 volumes of the spiritual teachings of various saints for meditation and prayer.

The Classics of Western Spirituality. New York: Paulist Press. This series contains over 130 volumes of the original writings of universally acknowledged teachers of the Catholic, Protestant, Eastern Orthodox, Jewish, Islamic, and Native American traditions.

Sister Kathleen Atkinson is a Benedictine Sister from the Annunciation Monastery in Bismarck, ND. Nationally recognized as a leader in hunger and homelessness education, she has developed service learning experiences for all age groups and led service teams to a variety of foreign and United States locations. After returning from time in Guatemala with the Institute for Trafficked, Exploited and Missing Persons, she is currently engaged in speaking, writing, and a "Ministry on the Margins" with at-risk youth, state-penitentiary inmates, and other people who are God's anawim among us. She is the author of *God Is Always There: Psalms for Every Moment* and a contributing writer to *The 5 W's of Our Catholic Faith* (both from Liguori Publications).